An Unentangled Knowing

An Unentangled Knowing

Lessons in Training the Mind

Upāsikā Kee Nanayon
(Acharn Kor Khao-suan-luang)

Translated from the Thai by
Thanissaro Bhikkhu

Buddhist Publication Society
Kandy • Sri Lanka

Published in 1996

Buddhist Publication Society
P.O. Box 61
54, Sangharaja Mawatha
Kandy, Sri Lanka

Copyright © 1995 Khao-suan-luang Dhamma Community

ISBN 955-24-0145-3

First published in 1995 by Dhamma Dana Publications (U.S.A.).
Published by the BPS with the permission of the translator and the
copyright holder.

Typeset at the BPS
Text set in Palatino

Printed in Sri Lanka by
Kanaratne & Sons Ltd.
Colombo 10

Contents

Contents

Upasika Kee Nanayon
(1901–1978)

Introduction

Upāsikā Kee Nanayon, also known by her pen name, Achan Kor Khao-suan-luang, was perhaps the foremost woman Dhamma teacher in twentieth-century Thailand. Born in 1901 to a Chinese merchant family in Rajburi, a town to the west of Bangkok, she was the eldest of five children—or, counting her father's children by a second wife, the eldest of eight. Her mother was a very religious woman and taught her the rudiments of Buddhist practice, such as nightly chants and the observance of the precepts, from an early age. In later life she described how, at the age of six, she became so filled with fear and loathing at the miseries her mother went through in being pregnant and giving birth to a younger sibling that, on seeing the newborn child for the first time—"sleeping quietly, a little red thing with black, black hair"—she ran away from home for three days. This experience, plus the anguish she must have felt when her parents separated, probably lay behind her decision, made when she was still quite young, never to submit to what she saw as the slavery of marriage.

During her teens she devoted her spare time to Dhamma books and to meditation, and her working hours to a small business to support her father in his old age. Her meditation progressed well enough that she was able to teach him meditation, with fairly good results, in the last year of his life. After his death she continued her business with the thought of saving up enough money to enable herself to live the remainder of her life in a secluded place and give herself fully to the practice. Her aunt and uncle, who were also interested in Dhamma practice, had a small home near a forested hill, Khao Suan Luang (RoyalPark Mountain), outside of Rajburi, where she often went to practice. In 1945, as life disrupted by World War II had begun to return to normal, she gave up her business, joined her aunt and uncle in moving to the hill, and there the three of them began a life devoted entirely to meditation. The small retreat they made for themselves in an abandoned monastic dwelling eventually grew to become the nucleus of a women's practice center that has flourished to this day.

Life at the retreat was frugal, in line with the fact that outside support was minimal in the early years. However, even now that the center has become well-known and established, the same frugal style has been maintained for its benefits in subduing greed, pride, and other mental defilements, as well as for the pleasure it offers in unburdening the heart. The women practicing at the center are all vegetarian and abstain from such stimulants as tobacco, coffee, tea, and betel nut. They meet daily for chanting, group meditation, and discussion of the practice. In the years when Upāsikā Kee's health was still strong, she would hold special meetings at which the members would report on their practice, after which she would give a talk touching on any important issues that had been brought up in their reports. Most of the talks recorded in this volume were given during sessions of this sort.

In the center's early years, small groups of friends and relatives would visit on occasion to give support and to listen to Upāsikā Kee's Dhamma talks. As word spread of the high standard of her teachings and practice, larger and larger groups came to visit, and more women began to join the community. When tape recording was introduced to Thailand in the mid-1950's, friends began recording her talks and, in 1956, a group of them printed a small volume of her transcribed talks for free distribution. By the mid-1960's, the stream of free Dhamma literature from Khao Suan Luang—Upāsikā Kee's poetry as well as her talks—had grown to a flood. This attracted even more people to her center and established her as one of the best-known Dhamma teachers, male or female, in Thailand.

Upāsikā Kee was something of an autodidact. Although she picked up the rudiments of meditation during her frequent visits to monasteries in her youth, she practiced mostly on her own without any formal study under a meditation teacher. Most of her instruction came from books—the Pali Canon and the works of contemporary teachers—and was tested in the crucible of her own relentless honesty. Her later teachings show the influence of the writings of Buddhadasa Bhikkhu, although she transformed his concepts in ways that made them entirely her own.

In the later years of her life she developed cataracts that eventually left her blind, but she still continued a rigorous schedule of meditating and receiving visitors interested in the Dhamma. She passed away quietly in 1978 after entrusting the center to a committee she appointed from among its members. Her younger sister, Upāsikā Wan, who up to that point had played a major role as supporter and facilitator for the center, joined the community within a few months of Upāsikā Kee's death and soon became its leader, a position she held until her death in 1993. Now the center is once again being run by committee and has grown to accommodate sixty members.

A Note on the Translations

With two exceptions, the passages translated here are taken from Upāsikā Kee's extemporaneous talks. The first exception is the prologue, excerpted from a poem she wrote on the twentieth anniversary of the founding of the center at Khao Suan Luang, reflecting on life at the center in its early years. The second exception is the first piece in Part I, a brief outline of the practice that she wrote as an introduction to one of her early volumes of talks.

All of the passages are translated directly from the Thai. Many have previously appeared in books privately printed in Thailand or published by the Buddhist Publication Society. Originally I had hoped to include all of her talks that have been translated into English, but one book of her talks— printed under the titles, *Directing to Self-Penetration* and *Directions for Insight*—was originally translated by another hand. A long search, conducted by Upāsikā Sumana Hengsawat in the Khao Suan Luang library, succeeded in uncovering the Thai originals for only four of the six talks in that volume, which are here translated in Part III. Seeing how far the earlier translations diverged from the Thai in those four, I abandoned the idea of including in this volume revised versions of the translations of the remaining two.

My aim in translation has been to adhere as closing as possible to the Thai, both in substance and in style. This has meant including a fair amount of repetition, but I have found that the repetition plays a large role in the forcefulness of Upāsikā Kee's presentation and so feel no qualms at leaving it in. The talks work especially well if read aloud.

THANISSARO BHIKKHU

Prologue

In 1965, soon after the death of her uncle, Upasika Kee wrote a long poem on the first 20 years at Khao Suan Luang. What follows is a prose paraphrase of some of its passages:

On June 26, 1945, the three of us—my aunt, uncle, and myself—first came to stay in the old meeting hall on Khao Suan Luang. Uncle Plien Raksae handled the repairs. He used to be a farmer living on the other side of the hill, but now he had left the worries of home to practice the Dhamma.

The place was an old monastic retreat that several monks had set up and then abandoned many years before. Next to the meeting hall was an octagonal cement tank to collect rain water from the roof of the hall—enough to last all year. Old meditation huts at distant intervals lined the path up the hill to the hall. Local lay people had dug a large pond at the foot of the hill to collect rain water, but it would dry up in the hot season. An old ox-cart track at the edge of the pond circled the hill, marking off an area of thirty acres that we decided to make our retreat.

When we first arrived, the place was all overgrown with bushes and weeds, so we had to clear paths through the forest and up the hill to the cave under the cliff face—a cave we called UttamaSanti, HighestPeace Cave. It was a lot of fun, clearing the forest day after day, and soon another woman joined us. In those days there were no visitors, so the place was very quiet.

When I first came I was afraid of ghosts and of people, but my resolve was firm, and my belief in *kamma* gradually lessened my worries and fears. I had never before lived in the forest. I hadn't seen any purpose in it before, and thought that it would be better to stay in the town, running a store and having enough money to last me the rest of my life. But coming to the forest and living very simply, I came to feel light-hearted and free. Seeing nature all around me inspired me to explore inside my own mind.

> With no struggling, no thinking,
> The mind, still,
> Will see cause and effect
> Vanishing in the Void.
> Attached to nothing, letting go:
> > Know that this is the way
> > to allay all stress.

For food, we lived off the delicious bamboo shoots that grew in the bamboo clusters at the top of the hill. The bitter fruits and berries that the trees produced during the rainy season provided our medicine. As for utensils, we used whatever we could find in the forest. Coconut shells, for instance, made excellent bowls: You didn't have to worry about their getting broken. We kept patching our old clothes and slept on old mats and wooden pillows in the meeting hall. Up in the cave I kept another wooden pillow to use when I rested there. Wooden pillows are ideal for meditators. If you use soft ones, you have to worry about storing them safely.

All sorts of animals lived around the hill: wildcats, rabbits, moles, lizards, snakes, wild fowl. Bands of monkeys would pester us from time to time when they came to eat the fruit off the trees. The calls of owls and mourning doves filled the air. Throngs of bats lived in the cave, flying out at night and returning just before dawn. As for the ants and termites, they couldn't fly, so they walked, so intent—going where? And what were they carrying with such active cooperation?

Introduction

Coming here, we cut off all thoughts of the past and thought only of making progress in our search for release from suffering. Visitors came and went, and more people came to stay, intent on instruction in strategies for training the mind, and their burdens of suffering would lessen. Never trained to teach, I now often found myself discussing the practice and skillful means for contemplating the five aggregates. All of those who came to practice had frequented monasteries before, so they were already well-educated in the Dhamma and approached the practice in a clear-eyed manner. We met frequently to discuss the many techniques to use in training the heart to explore the body and mind skillfully.

Now, after twenty years, the forest is no longer wild, and the place has been improved in numerous ways to make it more conducive to the practice for going beyond the cycle of suffering and stress. If we continue progressing in the path, following the example of the noble disciples—with sincerity, truth, and endurance in our efforts to explore the five aggregates intelligently—we are sure to see the results we hope for.

> Please help keep this forest fragrant
> Till earth and sky are no more,
> The forest of RoyalPark Hill,
> Still garden of calm
> Where the Dhamma resounds:
> > The Unbound—Nibbāna—
> > is a nature devoid
> > of all suffering.

PART I

Looking Inward

THE PRACTICE IN BRIEF

March 17, 1954

Those who practice the Dhamma should train themselves to understand in the following stages:

The training that is easy to learn, gives immediate results, and is suitable for every time, every place, for people of every age and either sex, is to study in the school of this body—a fathom long, a cubit wide, and a span thick—with its perceiving mind in charge. This body has many things, ranging from the crude to the subtle, that are well worth knowing.

The steps of the training:

1. To begin with, know that the body is composed of various physical properties, the major ones being the properties of earth, water, fire, and wind; the minor ones being the aspects that adhere to the major ones: things like color, smell, shape, etc.

These properties are unstable (inconstant), stressful, and unclean. If you look into them deeply, you will see that there's no substance to them at all. They are simply impersonal conditions, with nothing worth calling "me" or "mine." When you can clearly perceive the body in these terms, you will be able to let go of any clinging or attachment to it as an entity, your self, someone else, this or that.

9

2. The second step is to deal with mental phenomena (feelings, perceptions, thought-formations, and consciousness). Focus on keeping track of the truth that these are characterized by arising, persisting, and then disbanding. In other words, their nature is to arise and disband, arise and disband, repeatedly. When you investigate to see this truth, you will be able to let go of your attachments to mental phenomena as entities, as your self, someone else, this or that.

3. Training on the level of practice doesn't simply mean studying, listening, or reading. You have to practice so as to see clearly with your own mind in the following steps:

a. Start out by brushing aside all external concerns and turn to look inside at your own mind until you can know in what ways it is clear or murky, calm or unsettled. The way to do this is to have mindfulness and self-awareness in charge as you keep aware of the body and mind until you've trained the mind to stay firmly in a state of normalcy, i.e. neutrality.

b. Once the mind can stay in a state of normalcy, you will see mental formations or preoccupations in their natural state of arising and disbanding. The mind will be empty, neutral, and still—neither pleased nor displeased—and will see physical and mental phenomena as they arise and disband naturally, of their own accord.

c. When the knowledge that there is no self to any of these things becomes thoroughly clear, you will meet with something that lies further inside, beyond all suffering and stress, free from the cycles of change—deathless—free from birth as well as death, since all things that take birth must by nature age, grow ill, and die.

d. When you see this truth clearly, the mind will be empty, not holding onto anything. It won't even assume itself to be a mind or anything at all. In other words, it won't latch onto itself as being anything of any sort. All that remains is a pure condition of Dhamma.

e. Those who see this pure condition of Dhamma in full

clarity are bound to grow disenchanted with the repeated sufferings of life. When they know the truth of the world and the Dhamma throughout, they will see the results clearly, right in the present, *that there exists that which lies beyond all suffering.* They will know this without having to ask or take it on faith from anyone, for the Dhamma is *paccattaṁ,* i.e. something really to be known for oneself. Those who have seen this truth within themselves will attest to it always.

AN HOUR'S MEDITATION

March 3, 1977

For those of you who have never sat in meditation, here is how it's done: Fold your legs, one on top of the other, but don't cut off the nerves or the blood flow, or else the breath energy in your legs will stagnate and cause you pain. Sit straight and place your hands, one on top of the other, on your lap. Hold your head up straight and keep your back straight, too—as if you had a yardstick sticking down your spine. You have to work at keeping it straight, you know. Don't spend the time slouching down and then stretching up again, or else the mind won't be able to settle down and be still....

Keep the body straight and your mindfulness firm—firmly with the breath. However coarse or refined your breath may be, simply breathe in naturally. You don't have to force the breath or tense your body. Simply breathe in and out in a relaxed way. Only then will the mind begin to settle down. As soon as the breath grows normally refined and the mind has begun to settle down, focus your attention on the mind itself. If it slips off elsewhere, or any thoughts come in to intrude, simply know right there at the mind. Know the mind

11

right at the mind with every in-and-out breath for the entire hour....

When you focus on the breath, using the breath as a leash to tie the mind in place so that it doesn't go wandering off, you have to use your endurance. That is, you have to endure pain. For example, when you sit for a long time there's going to be pain, because you've never sat for so long before. So first make sure that you keep the mind normal and neutral. When pain arises, don't focus on the pain. Let go of it as much as you can. Let go of it and focus on your mind.... For those of you who've never done this before, it may take a while. Whenever any pain or anything arises, if the mind is affected by craving or defilement, it'll struggle because it doesn't want the pain. All it wants is pleasure.

This is where you have to be patient and endure the pain, *because pain is something that has to occur.* If there's pleasure, don't get enthralled with it. If there's pain, don't push it away. Start out by keeping the mind neutral as your basic stance. Then whenever pleasure or pain arises, don't get pleased or upset. Keep the mind continuously neutral and figure out how to let go. If there's a lot of pain, you first have to endure it and then relax your attachments. Don't think of the pain as being *your* pain. Let it be the pain of the body, the pain of nature.

If the mind latches tightly onto anything, it really suffers. It struggles. So here we patiently endure and let go. You have to practice so that you're really good at handling pain. If you can let go of physical pain, you'll be able to let go of all sorts of other sufferings and pains as well.... Keep watching the pain, knowing the pain, letting it go. Once you can let it go, you don't have to use a lot of endurance. It takes a lot of endurance only at the beginning. Once the pain arises, separate the mind from it. Let it be the pain of the body. Don't let the mind be pained, too....

This is something that requires equanimity. If you can maintain equanimity in the face of pleasure or pain, it can make the mind peaceful—peaceful even though the pain is still pain. The mind keeps knowing, enduring the pain so as to let it go.

After you've worked at this a good while, you'll come to see how important the ways of the mind are. The mind may be hard to train, but if you keep training it—if you have the time, you can practice at home, at night or early in the morning, keeping watch on your mind—you'll gain the understanding that comes from mindfulness and discernment. Those who don't train the mind like this go through life—birth, ageing, illness, and death—not knowing a thing about the mind at all.

When you know your own mind, then when any really heavy illness comes along, the fact that you know your mind will make the pain less and less. But this is something you have to work at doing correctly. It's not easy, yet once the mind is well trained there's no match for it. It can do away with pain and suffering, and doesn't get restless and agitated. It grows still and cool—refreshed and blooming right there within itself. So try to experience this still, quiet mind....

This is a really important skill to develop, because it will make craving, defilement, and attachment grow weaker and weaker. We all have defilements, you know. Greed, anger, and delusion cloud all of our hearts. If we haven't trained ourselves in meditation, our hearts are constantly burning with suffering and stress. Even the pleasure we feel over external things is pleasure only in half-measures, because there's suffering and stress in the delusion that thinks it's pleasure. As for the pleasure that comes from the practice, it's a cool pleasure that lets go of everything, really free from any sense of "me" or "mine." I ask that you reach the Dhamma that's the real meat inside this thing undisturbed by defilement, undisturbed by pain or anything else.

Even though there's pain in the body, you have to figure out how to let it go. The body is simply the four elements—

earth, water, wind, and fire. It has to keep showing its inconstancy and stressfulness, so keep your mindfulness neutral, at equanimity. Let the mind be above its feelings—above pleasure, above pain, above everything....

All it really takes is endurance—endurance and relinquishment, letting things go, seeing that they're not us, not ours. This is a point you have to hammer at, over and over again. When we say you have to endure, you *really* have to endure. Don't be willing to surrender. Craving is going to keep coming up and whispering—telling you to change things, to try for this or that kind of pleasure—but don't you listen to it. You have to listen to the Buddha—the Buddha who tells you to let go of craving. Otherwise, craving will plaster and paint things over; the mind will struggle and won't be able to settle down. So you have to give it your all. Look at this hour as a special hour—special in that you're using special endurance *to keep watch on your own heart and mind.*

A BASIC ORDER IN LIFE

January 29, 1964

The most important thing in the daily life of a person who practices the Dhamma is to keep to the precepts and to care for them more than you care for your life—to maintain them in a way that the Noble Ones would praise. If you don't have this sort of regard for the precepts, then the vices that run counter to them will become your everyday habits....

Meditators who see that the breaking of a precept is something trifling and insignificant spoil their entire practice. If you can't practice even these basic, beginning levels of the Dhamma, you will ruin all the qualities you'll be trying to develop in the later stages of the practice. This is why you have to stick to the precepts as your basic foundation and to keep a lookout for anything in your behavior that falls short of them. Only then will you be able to benefit from your practice for the sake of eliminating your sufferings with greater and greater precision.

If you simply act in line with the cravings and desires swelling out of the sense of self that has no fear of the fires of defilement, you'll have to suffer both in this life and in lives to come. If you don't have a sense of conscience—a sense of shame at the thought of doing shoddy actions, and a fear of their consequences—your practice can only deteriorate day by day....

When people live without any order to their lives—without even the basic order that comes with the precepts—there's no way they can attain purity. We have to examine ourselves: In what ways at present are we breaking our precepts in thought, word, or deed? If we simply let things pass and aren't intent on examining ourselves to see the harm that comes from breaking the precepts and following the defilements, our practice can only sink lower and lower. Instead of extinguishing defilements and suffering, it will simply succumb to the power of craving. If this is the case, what damage is done? How much freedom does the mind lose? These are things we have to learn for ourselves. When we do, our practice of self-inspection in higher matters will get solid results and won't go straying off into nonsense. For this reason, whenever craving or defilement shows itself in any way in any of our actions, we have to catch hold of it and examine what's going on inside the mind.

Once we're aware with real mindfulness and discernment, we'll see the poison and power of the defilements. We'll feel disgust for them and want to extinguish them as much as we can. But if we use our defilements to examine things, they'll say everything is fine. The same as when we're predisposed to liking a certain person: Even if he acts badly, we say he's good. If he acts wrongly, we say he's right. This is the way the defilements are. They say that everything we do is right and throw all the blame on other people, other things. So we can't trust it—this sense of "self" in which craving and defilement lord it over the heart. We can't trust it at all....

The violence of defilement, or this sense of self, is like that of a fire burning a forest or burning a house. It won't listen to anyone, but simply keeps burning away, burning away inside of you. And that's not all. It's always out to set fire to other people, too.

The fires of suffering, the fires of defilement consume all those who don't contemplate themselves or who don't have any means of practice for putting them out. People of this sort can't withstand the power of the defilements, can't help but follow along wherever their cravings lead them. The moment they're provoked, they follow in line with these things. This is why the sensations in the mind when provoked by defilement are very important, for they can lead you to do things with no sense of shame, no fear for the consequences of doing evil at all—which means that you're sure to break your precepts.

Once you've followed the defilements, they feel really satisfied—like arsonists who feel gleeful when they've set other people's places on fire. As soon as you've called somebody something vile or spread some malicious gossip, the defilements really like it. Your sense of self really likes it, because acting in line with defilement like that gives it real satisfaction. As a consequence, it keeps filling itself with the vices that run counter to the precepts, falling into hell in this very lifetime without realizing it. So take a good look at the violence the defilements do to you, to see whether you should keep socializing with them, to see whether you should regard them as your friends or your enemies....

As soon as any wrong views or ideas come out of the mind,

we have to analyze them and turn around so as to catch sight of the facts within us. No matter what issues the defilements raise, focusing on the faults of others, we have to turn around and look within. *When we realize our own faults and can come to our senses:* That's where our study of the Dhamma, our practice of the Dhamma, shows its real rewards.

CONTINUOUS PRACTICE

January 14, 1964

The passage for reflection on the four requisites (clothing, food, shelter, and medicine) is a fine pattern for contemplation, but we never actually get down to putting it to use. We're taught to memorize it in the beginning not simply to pass the time of day or so that we can talk about it every now and then, but so that we can use it to contemplate the requisites until we really know them with our own mindfulness and discernment. If we actually get down to contemplating in line with the established pattern, our minds will become much less influenced by unwise thoughts. But it's the rare person who genuinely makes this a continuous practice.... For the most part we're not interested. We don't feel like contemplating this sort of thing. We'd much rather contemplate whether this or that food will taste good or not, and if it doesn't taste good, how to fix it so that it will. That's the sort of thing we like to contemplate.

Try to see the filthiness of food and of the physical properties in general, to see their emptiness of any real entity or self. There's nothing of any substance to the physical properties of the body, which are all rotten and decomposing. The body is like a restroom over a cesspool. We can decorate it on

17

the outside to make it pretty and attractive, but on the inside it's full of the most horrible, filthy things. Whenever we excrete anything, we ourselves are repelled by it; yet even though we're repelled by it, it's there inside us, in our intestines—decomposing, full of worms, awful smelling. There's just the flimsiest membrane covering it up, yet we fall for it and hold tight to it. We don't see the constant decomposition of this body, in spite of the filth and smells it sends out....

The reason we're taught to memorize the passage for reflecting on the requisites, and to use it to contemplate, is so that we'll see the inconstancy of the body, to see that there's no "self" to any of it or to any of the mental phenomena we sense with every moment.

We contemplate mental phenomena to see clearly that they're not-self, to see this with every moment. The moments of the mind—the arising, persisting, and disbanding of mental sensations—are very subtle and fast. To see them, the mind has to be quiet. If the mind is involved in distractions, thoughts, and imaginings, we won't be able to penetrate in to see its characteristics as it deals with its objects, to see what the arising and disbanding within it is like.

This is why we have to practice concentration: to make the mind quiet, to provide a foundation for our contemplation. For instance, you can focus on the breath, or be aware of the mind as it focuses on the breath. Actually, when you focus on the breath, you're also aware of the mind. And again, the mind is what knows the breath. So you focus exclusively on the breath together with the mind. Don't think of anything else, and the mind will settle down and grow still. Once it attains stillness on this level, you've got your chance to contemplate.

Making the mind still so that you can contemplate it is something you have to keep working at in the beginning. The same holds true with training yourself to be mindful and fully aware

in all your activities. This is something you really have to
work at continuously in this stage, something you have to do
all the time. At the same time, you have to arrange the external conditions of your life so that you won't have any concerns to distract you....

Now, of course, the practice is something you can do in
any set of circumstances—for example, when you come home
from work you can sit and meditate for a while—but when
you're trying seriously to make it continuous, to make it habitual, it's much more difficult than that. "Making it habitual"
means being fully mindful and aware with each in-and-out
breath, wherever you go, whatever you do, whether you're
healthy, sick, or whatever, and regardless of what happens
inside or out. *The mind has to be in a state of all-encompassing
awareness while keeping track of the arising and disbanding of mental
phenomena at all times*—to the point where you can stop the
mind from forming thoughts under the power of craving and
defilement the way it used to before you began the practice.

EVERY IN-AND-OUT BREATH

January 29, 1964

Try keeping your awareness with the breath to see what the
still mind is like. It's very simple, all the rules have been laid
out, but when you actually try to do it, something resists. It's
hard. But when you let your mind think 108 or 1009 things,
no matter what, it's all easy. It's not hard at all. *Try and see if
you can engage your mind with the breath in the same way it's
been engaged with the defilements.* Try engaging it with the breath
and see what happens. See if you can disperse the defilements

19

with every in-and-out breath. Why is it that the mind can stay engaged with the defilements all day long and yet go for entire days without knowing how heavy or subtle the breath is at all?

So try and be observant. The bright, clear awareness that stems from staying focused on the mind at all times: Sometimes a strong sensory contact comes and can make it blur and fade away with no trouble at all. But if you can keep hold of the breath as a reference point, that state of mind can be more stable and sure, more insured. It has two fences around it. If there's only one fence, it can easily break.

TAKING A STANCE

January 14, 1964

Normally the mind isn't willing to stop and look, to stop and know itself, which is why we have to keep training it continually so that it will settle down from its restlessness and grow still. Let your desires and thought-processes settle down. Let the mind take its stance in a state of normalcy, not liking or disliking anything. To reach a basic level of emptiness and freedom, you first have to take a stance. If you don't have a stance against which to measure things, progress will be very difficult. If your practice is hit-or-miss—a bit of that, a little of this—you won't get any results. So the mind first has to take a stance.

When you take a stance that the mind can maintain in a state of normalcy, don't go slipping off into the future. Have the mind know itself in the stance of the present: "Right now it's in a state of normalcy. No likes or dislikes have arisen yet. It hasn't created any issues. It's not being disturbed by a desire for this or that."

Then look on in to the basic level of the mind to see if it's as normal and empty as it should be. If you're really looking inside, really aware inside, then *that which is looking and knowing is mindfulness and discernment in and of itself.* You don't need to search for anything anywhere else to come and do your looking for you. As soon as you stop to look, stop to know whether or not the mind is in a state of normalcy, then if it's normal you'll know immediately that it's normal. If it's not, you'll know immediately that it's not.

Take care to keep this awareness going. If you can keep knowing like this continuously, the mind will be able to keep its stance continuously as well. As soon as the thought occurs to you to check things out, you'll immediately stop to look, stop to know, without any need to go searching for knowledge from anywhere else. You look, you know, right there at the mind and can tell whether or not it's empty and still. Once you see that it is, then you investigate to see *how* it's empty, *how* it's still. It's not the case that once it's empty, that's the end of the matter; once it's still, that's the end of the matter. *That's not the case at all.* You have to keep watch of things, you have to investigate at all times. Only then will you see the changing—the arising and disbanding—occurring in that emptiness, that stillness, that state of normalcy.

THE DETAILS OF PAIN

December 28, 1972

To lead your daily life by keeping constant supervision over the mind is a way of learning what life is for. It's a way of learning how we can act so as to rid ourselves more and more of suffering and stress—because the suffering and stress caused by defilement, attachment, and craving are sure to take all sorts of forms. Only by being aware with true mindfulness and discernment can we comprehend them for what they are. Otherwise, we'll simply live obliviously, going wherever events will lead us. This is why mindfulness and discernment are tools for reading yourself, for testing yourself within so that you won't be careless or complacent, oblivious to the fact that suffering is basically what life is all about.

This point is something we really have to comprehend so that we can live without being oblivious. The pains and discontent that fill our bodies and minds all show us the truths of inconstancy, stress, and not-selfness within us. If you contemplate what's going on inside until you can get down to the details, you'll see the truths that appear within and without, all of which come down to inconstancy, stress, and not-selfness. But the delusion basic to our nature will see everything wrongly—as constant, easeful, and self—and so make us live obliviously, even though there is nothing to guarantee how long our lives will last.

Our dreams and delusions make us forget that we live in the midst of a mass of pain and stress—the stress of defilements, the pain of birth. Birth, ageing, illness, and death: All these are painful and stressful, in the midst of instability and change. They're things we have no control over, for they must circle around in line with the laws of *kamma* and the defilements we've been amassing all along. Life that floats along in the round of rebirth is thus nothing but stress and pain.

If we can find a way to develop our mindfulness and discernment, they'll be able to cut the round of rebirth so that we won't have to keep wandering on. They'll help us know that birth is painful, ageing is painful, illness is painful, death is painful, and that these are all things that defilement, attachment, and craving keep driving through the cycles of change.

So as long as we have the opportunity, we should study the truths appearing throughout our body and mind, and we'll come to know that the elimination of stress and pain, the elimination of defilement, is a function of our practice of the Dhamma. If we don't practice the Dhamma, we'll keep floating along in the round of rebirth that is so drearily repetitious —repetitious in its birth, ageing, illness, and death, driven on by defilement, attachment, and craving, causing us repeated stress, repeated pain. Living beings for the most part don't know where these stresses and pains come from or what they come from, because they've never studied them, never contemplated them, so they stay stupid and deluded, wandering on and on without end....

If we can stop and be still, the mind will have a chance to be free, to contemplate its sufferings, and to let them go. This will give it a measure of peace, because it will no longer want anything out of the round of rebirth—for it sees that there's nothing lasting to it, that it's simply stress over and over again. Whatever you grab hold of is stress. This is why you need mindfulness and discernment to know and see things for yourself, so that you can supervise the mind and keep it calm, without letting it fall victim to temptation.

This practice is something of the highest importance. People who don't study or practice the Dhamma have wasted their birth as human beings, because they're born deluded and simply stay deluded. But if we study the Dhamma, we'll become wise to suffering and know the path of practice for freeing ourselves from it....

Once we follow the right path, the defilements won't be able to drag us around, won't be able to burn us, because *we're* the ones burning *them* away. We'll come to realize that the more we can burn them away, the more strength of mind we'll gain. If we let the defilements burn us, the mind will be sapped of its strength, which is why this is something you have to be very careful about. Keep trying to burn away the defilements in your every activity, and you'll be storing up strength for your mindfulness and discernment so that they'll be brave in dealing with all sorts of suffering and pain.

You must come to see the world as nothing but stress. There's no real ease to it at all. The awareness we gain from mindfulness and discernment will make us disenchanted with life in the world because it will see things for what they are in every way, both within us and without.

The entire world is nothing but an affair of delusion, an affair of suffering. People who don't know the Dhamma, who don't practice the Dhamma—no matter what their status or position in life—lead deluded, oblivious lives. When they fall ill or are about to die, they're bound to suffer enormously because they haven't taken the time to understand the defilements that burn their hearts and minds in everyday life. Yet if we make a constant practice of studying and contemplating ourselves as our everyday activity, it will help free us from all sorts of suffering and distress. And when this is the case, how can we *not* want to practice?

Only intelligent people, though, will be able to stick with the practice. Foolish people won't want to bother. They'd much rather follow the defilements than burn them away. To practice the Dhamma you need a certain basic level of intelligence—enough to have seen at least *something* of the stresses and sufferings that come from defilement. Only then can your practice progress. And no matter how difficult it gets, you'll have to keep practicing on to the end.

This practice isn't something you do from time to time, you know. You have to keep at it continuously throughout life. Even if it involves so much physical pain or mental anguish that tears are bathing your cheeks, you have to keep with the chaste life because you're playing for real. If you don't follow the chaste life, you'll get mired in heaps of suffering and flame. So you have to learn your lessons from pain. Try to contemplate it until you can understand it and let it go, and you'll gain one of life's greatest rewards.

Don't think that you were born to gain this or that level of comfort. You were born to study pain and the causes of pain, and to follow the practice that frees you from pain. This is the most important thing there is. Everything else is trivial and unimportant. What's important all lies with the practice.

Don't think that the defilements will go away easily. When they don't come in blatant forms, they come in subtle ones— and the dangers of the subtle ones are hard to see. Your contemplation will have to be subtle, too, if you want to get rid of them. You'll come to realize that this practice of the Dhamma, in which we contemplate to get to the details inside us, is like sharpening our tools so that, when stress and suffering arise, we can weaken them and cut them away. If your mindfulness and discernment are brave, the defilements will have to lose out to them. But if you don't train your mindfulness and discernment to be brave, the defilements will crush you to pieces.

We were born to do battle with the defilements and to strengthen our mindfulness and discernment. We'll find that the worth of our practice will grow higher and higher because in our everyday life we've done continuous battle with the stresses and pains caused by defilement, craving, and temptation all along—so that the defilements will grow thin and our mindfulness and discernment stronger. We'll sense within ourselves that the mind isn't as troubled and restless as it used to be. It's grown peaceful and calm. The stresses and sufferings of defilement, attachment, and craving have grown weaker. Even though we haven't yet wiped them out completely, they've grown continually weaker—because we don't feed them. We don't give them shelter. We do what we can to weaken them so that they grow thinner and thinner each time.

And we have to be brave in contemplating stress and pain, because when we don't feel any great suffering we tend to get complacent. But when the pains and sufferings in our body and mind grow sharp and biting, we have to use our mindfulness and discernment to be strong. *Don't let your*

25

spirits be weak. Only then will you be able to do away with your sufferings and pains.

We have to learn our lessons from pain so that ultimately the mind can gain its freedom from it, instead of being weak and losing out to it all of the time. We have to be brave in doing battle with it to the ultimate extreme—until we reach the point where we can let it go. Pain is something always present in this conglomerate of body and mind. It's here for us to see with every moment. If we contemplate it till we know all its details, we can then make it our sport: seeing that the pain is the pain of natural conditions and not *our* pain. This is something we have to research so as to get to the details: *that it's not our pain,* it's the pain of the aggregates [form, feeling, perception, thought-formations, and consciousness]. Knowing in this way means that we can separate out the properties—the properties of matter and those of the mind—to see how they interact with one another, how they change. It's something really fascinating.... Watching pain is a way of building up lots of mindfulness and discernment.

But if you focus on pleasure and ease, you'll simply stay deluded like people in general. They get carried away with the pleasure that comes from watching or listening to the things they like—but then when pain comes to their bodies and minds to the point where tears are bathing their cheeks, think of how much they suffer! And then they have to be parted from their loved ones, which makes it even worse. But those of us who practice the Dhamma don't need to be deluded like that, because we know and see with every moment that only stress arises, only stress persists, only stress passes away. Aside from stress, nothing arises; aside from stress, nothing passes away. This is there for us to perceive with every moment. If we contemplate it, we'll see it.

So we can't let ourselves be oblivious. This is what the truth is, and we have to study it so as to know it—especially in our life of the practice. We have to contemplate stress all the time to see its every manifestation. The arahants live without being oblivious because they know the truth at all times, and their hearts are clean and pure. As for us with our defilements, we have to keep trying, because if we continually supervise the mind with mindfulness and discernment, we'll be able to keep the defilements from making it dirty and obscured. Even if it does become obscured in any way, we'll be able to remove that obscurity and make the mind empty and free.

This is the practice that weakens all the defilements, attachments, and cravings within us. It's because of this practice of the Dhamma that our lives will become free. So I ask you to keep working at the practice without being complacent, because if in whatever span of life is left to you, you keep trying to the full extent of your abilities, you'll gain the mindfulness and discernment to see the facts within yourself, and be able to let go—free from any sense of self, free from any sense of self—continuously.

AWARE RIGHT AT AWARENESS

November 3, 1975

The mind, if mindfulness and awareness are watching over it, won't meet with any suffering as the result of its actions. If suffering *does* arise, we'll be immediately aware of it and able to put it out. This is one point of the practice we can work at constantly. And we can test ourselves by seeing how refined and subtle our all-around awareness is inside the mind. Whenever the mind slips away and goes out to receive external sensory contact: Can it maintain its basic stance of mindfulness or internal awareness? The practice we need to work at in our everyday life is to have constant mindfulness, constant all-around present awareness like this. This is something we work at in every posture: sitting, standing, walking, and lying down. Make sure that your mindfulness stays continuous.

Living in this world—the mental and physical phenomena of these five aggregates—gives us plenty to contemplate. We must try to watch them, to contemplate them, so that we can understand them—because the truths we must learn how to read in this body and mind are here to be read with every moment. We don't have to get wrapped up with any other extraneous themes, because all the themes we need are right here in the body and mind. As long as we can keep the mind constantly aware all around, we can contemplate them.

If you contemplate mental and physical events to see how they arise and disband right in the here and now, and don't get involved with external things—like sights making contact with the eyes, or sounds with the ears—then there really aren't a lot of issues. The mind can be at normalcy, at equilibrium—calm and undisturbed by defilement or the stresses that come from sensory contact. It can look after itself and maintain its balance. You'll come to sense that if you're aware right at awareness in and of itself, without going out to get involved in external things like the mental labels and thoughts that will tend to arise, the mind will see their constant arising and disbanding—and won't be embroiled in anything. This way it can be disengaged, empty, and free. But if it goes out to label things as good or evil, as "me" or "mine," or gets attached to anything, it'll become unsettled and disturbed.

You have to know that if the mind can be still, totally and presently aware, and capable of contemplating with every activity, then blatant forms of suffering and stress will dissolve away. Even if they start to form, you can be alert to them and disperse them immediately. Once you see this actually happening—even in only the beginning stages—it can disperse a lot of the confusion and turmoil in your heart. In other words, don't let yourself dwell on the past or latch onto thoughts of the future. As for the events arising and passing away in the present, you have to leave them alone. Whatever your duties, simply do them as you have to—and the mind won't get worked up about anything. It will be able, to at least some extent, to be empty and still.

This one thing is something you have to be very careful about. You have to see this for yourself: *that if your mindfulness and discernment are constantly in charge, the truths of the arising and disbanding of mental and physical phenomena are always there for you to see,* always there for you to know. If you look at the body, you'll have to see it simply as physical properties. If you look at feelings, you'll have to see them as changing and inconstant: pleasure, pain, neither pleasure nor pain. To see these things is to see the truth within yourself. Don't let yourself get caught up with your external duties. Simply keep watch in this way inside. If your awareness is the sort that lets you read yourself correctly, the mind will be able to stay at normalcy, at equilibrium, at stillness, without any resistance.

If the mind can stay with itself and not go out looking for things to criticize or latch onto, it can maintain a natural form of stillness. So this is something we have to try for in our every activity. Keep your conversations to a minimum, and there won't be a whole lot of issues. Keep watch right at the mind. When you keep watch at the mind and your mindfulness is continuous, your senses can stay restrained.

Being mindful to keep watch in this way is something you have to work at. Try it and see: Can you keep this sort of awareness continuous? What sort of things can still get the mind engaged? What sorts of thoughts and labels of good and bad, me and mine, does it think up? Then look to see if these things arise and disband.

The sensations that arise from external contact and internal contact all have the same sorts of characteristics. You have to look till you can see this. If you know how to look, you'll see it—and the mind will grow calm.

So the point we have to practice in this latter stage doesn't have a whole lot of issues. There's nothing you have to do, nothing you have to label, nothing you have to think a whole lot about. Simply look carefully and contemplate, and in this very lifetime you'll have a chance to be calm and at peace, to know yourself more profoundly within. You'll come to see that the Dhamma is amazing *right here in your own heart.* Don't go searching for the Dhamma outside, for it lies within. Peace lies within, but we have to contemplate so that we're aware all around—subtly, deep down. If you look just on the surface, you won't understand anything. Even if the mind is at normalcy on the ordinary, everyday level, you won't understand much of anything at all.

You have to contemplate so that you're aware all around in a skillful way. The word "skillful" is something you can't explain with words, but you can know for yourself when you see the way in which awareness within the heart becomes special, when you see what this special awareness is about. This is something you can know for yourself.

And there's not really much to it: simply arising, persisting, disbanding. Look until this becomes plain—really, really plain—and everything disappears. All suppositions, all conventional formulations, all those aggregates and properties get swept away, leaving nothing but awareness pure and simple, not involved with anything at all—and there's nothing you have to do to it. Simply stay still and watch, be aware, letting go with every moment.

Simply watching this one thing is enough to do away with all sorts of defilements, all sorts of suffering and stress. If you don't know how to watch it, the mind is sure to get disturbed. It's sure to label things and concoct thoughts. As soon as there's contact at the senses, it'll go looking for things to latch onto, liking and disliking the objects it meets in the present and then getting involved with the past and future, spinning a web to entangle itself.

If you truly look at each moment in the present, there's really nothing at all. You'll see with every mental moment that things disband, disband, disband—really nothing at all. The important point is that you don't go forming issues out of nothing. The physical elements perform their duties in line with their elementary physical nature. The mental elements keep sensing in line with their own affairs. But our stupidity is what goes looking for issues to cook up, to label, to think about. It goes looking for things to latch onto and then gets the mind into a turmoil. This point is all we really have to see for ourselves. This is the problem we have to solve for ourselves. If things are left to their nature, pure and simple, there's no "us," no "them." This is a singular truth that will arise for us to know and see. There's nothing else we can know or see that can match it in any way. Once you know and see this one thing, it extinguishes all suffering and stress. The mind will be empty and free, with no meanings, no attachments, for anything at all.

This is why looking inward is so special in so many ways. Whatever arises, simply stop still to look at it. Don't get excited by it. If you become excited when any special intuitions arise when the mind is still, you'll get the mind worked up into a turmoil. If you become afraid that this or that will happen, that too will get you in a turmoil. So you have to stop and look, stop and know. The first thing is simply to look. The first thing is simply to know. And don't latch onto what you know—because whatever it is, it's simply a phenomenon that arises and disbands, arises and disbands, changing as part of its nature.

So your awareness has to take a firm stance right at the mind in and of itself. In the beginning stages, you have to know that when mindfulness is standing firm, the mind won't be affected by the objects of sensory contact. Keep working at maintaining this stance, holding firm to this stance. If you gain a sense of this for yourself, really knowing and seeing for yourself, your mindfulness will become even more firm. If anything arises in any way at all, you'll be able to let it go—and all the many troubles and turmoils of the mind will dissolve away.

If mindfulness slips and the mind goes out giving meanings to anything, latching onto anything, troubles will arise, so you have to keep checking on this with every moment. There's nothing else that's so worth checking on. You have to keep check on the mind in and of itself, contemplating the mind in and of itself. Or else you can contemplate the body in and of itself, feelings in and of themselves, or the phenomenon of arising and disbanding—i.e., the Dhamma—in and of itself. All of these things are themes you can keep track of entirely within yourself. You don't have to keep track of a lot of themes, because having a lot of themes is what will make you restless and distracted. First you'll practice this theme, then you'll practice that, then you'll make comparisons, all of which will keep the mind from growing still.

If you can take your stance at awareness, if you're skilled at looking, the mind can be at peace. You'll know how things arise and disband. First practice keeping awareness right within yourself so that your mindfulness can be firm, without being affected by the objects of sensory contact, so that it won't label things as good or bad, pleasing or displeasing. You have to keep checking to see that when the mind can be at normalcy, centered and neutral as its primary stance, then—whatever it knows or sees—it will be able to contemplate and let go.

The sensations in the mind that we explain at such length are still on the level of labels. Only when there can be *awareness right at awareness* will you really be able to know that the mind that is aware of awareness in this way doesn't send its knowing outside of this awareness. There are no issues. Noth-

ing can be concocted in the mind when it knows in this way.
In other words:

> An inward-staying
>   unentangled knowing,
> All outward-going knowing
>   cast aside.

The only thing you have to work at maintaining is the state
of mind at normalcy—knowing, seeing, and still in the present.
If you don't maintain it, if you don't keep looking after it,
then when sensory contact comes it will have an effect. The
mind will go out with labels of good and bad, liking and
disliking. So make sure you maintain the basic awareness
that's aware right at yourself. And don't let there be any
labeling. No matter what sort of sensory contact comes, you
have to make sure that this awareness comes first.

If you train yourself correctly in this way, everything will
stop. You won't go straying out through your senses of sight,
hearing, etc. The mind will stop and look, stop and be aware
right at awareness, so as to know the truth that all things
arise and disband. There's no real truth to anything. Only
our stupidity is what latches onto things, giving them meanings and then suffering for it—suffering because of its ignorance, suffering because of its unacquaintance with the five
aggregates—form, feelings, perceptions, thought-formations,
and consciousness—all of which are inconstant, stressful, and
not-self.

Use mindfulness to gather your awareness together, and
the mind will stop getting unsettled, stop running after things.
It will be able to stop and be still. Then make it know in this
way, see in this way *constantly*—at every moment, with every
activity. Work at watching and knowing the mind in and of
itself: That will be enough to cut away all sorts of issues. You
won't have to concern yourself with them.

If the body is in pain, simply keep watch of it. You can simply keep watch of feelings in the body because the mind that's aware of itself in this way can keep watch of anything within or without. Or it can simply be aware of itself to the point where it lets go of things outside, lets go of sensory contact, and keeps constant watch on the mind in and of itself. That's when you'll know that this is what the mind is like when it's at peace: It doesn't give meanings to anything. It's the emptiness of the mind unattached, uninvolved, unconcerned with anything at all.

These words—unattached, uninvolved, and unconcerned—are things you have to consider carefully, because what they refer to is subtle and deep. "Uninvolved" means uninvolved with sensory contact, undisturbed by the body or feelings. "Unconcerned" means not worried about past, future, or present. You have to contemplate these things until you know them skillfully. Even though they're subtle, you have to contemplate them until you know them thoroughly. And don't go concerning yourself with external things, because they'll keep you unsettled, keep you running, keep you distracted with labels and thoughts of good and bad and all that sort of thing. You have to put a stop to these things. If you don't, your practice won't accomplish anything, because these things keep playing up to you and deceiving you—i.e., once you see anything, it will fool you into seeing it as right, wrong, good, bad, and so forth.

Eventually you have to come down to the awareness that everything simply arises, persists, and then disbands. *Make sure you stay focused on the disbanding.* If you watch just the arising, you may get carried off on a tangent, but if you focus on the disbanding you'll see emptiness: Everything is disbanding every instant. No matter what you look at, no matter what you see, it's there for just an instant and then disbands. Then it arises again. Then it disbands. There's simply arising, knowing, disbanding.

So let's watch what happens of its own accord—because the arising and disbanding that occurs by way of the senses is something that happens of its own accord. You can't prevent it. You can't force it. If you look and know it without attachment, there will be none of the harm that comes from joy or sorrow. The mind will stay in relative normalcy and neutrality. But if you're forgetful and start latching on, labeling things in pairs in any way at all—good and bad, happy and sad, pleasing and displeasing—the mind will become unsettled: no longer empty, no longer still. When this happens, you have to probe on in to know why.

All the worthless issues that arise in the mind have to be cut away. Then you'll find that you have less and less to say, less and less to talk about, less and less to think about. These things grow less and less on their own. They stop on their own. But if you get involved in a lot of issues, the mind won't be able to stay still. *So we have to keep watching things that are completely worthless and without substance,* to see that they're not-self. Keep watching them repeatedly, because your awareness, coupled with the mindfulness and discernment that will know the truth, has to see that, "This isn't my self. There's no substance or worth to it at all. It simply arises and disbands right here. It's here for just an instant and then it disbands."

All we have to do is stop and look, stop and know clearly in this way, and we'll be able to do away with many, many kinds of suffering and stress. The normal stress of the aggregates will still occur—we can't prevent it—but we'll know that it's the stress of nature and won't latch onto it as ours.

So we keep watch of things that happen on their own. If we know how to watch, we keep watching things that happen on their own. Don't latch onto them as being you or yours. Keep this awareness firmly established in itself, as much as you can, and there won't be much else you'll have to remember or think about.

When you keep looking, keep knowing like this at all times,

you'll come to see that there are no big issues going on. There's just the issue of arising, persisting, and disbanding. You don't have to label anything as good or bad. If you simply look in this way, it's no great weight on the heart. But if you go dragging in issues of good and bad, self and all that, then suffering starts in a big way. The defilements start in a big way and weigh on the heart, making it troubled and upset. So you have to stop and look, stop and investigate really deep down inside. It's like water covered with duckweed: Only when we take our hand to part the duckweed and take a look will we see that the water beneath it is crystal clear.

As you look into the mind, you have to part it, you have to stop: stop thinking, stop labeling things as good or bad, stop everything. You can't go branding anything. Simply keep looking, keep knowing. When the mind is quiet, you'll see that there's nothing there. Everything is all still. Everything has all stopped inside. But as soon as there's labeling, even in the stillness, the stopping, the quiet, it will set things in motion. And as soon as things get set into motion, and you don't know how to let go right from the start, issues will arise, waves will arise. Once there are issues and waves, they strike the mind and it goes splashing all out of control. This splashing of the mind includes craving and defilement as well, because *avijjā*—ignorance—lies at its root....

Our major obstacle is this aggregate of perceptions, of labels. If we aren't aware of the arising and disbanding of perceptions, these labels will take hold. Perceptions are the chief instigators that label things within and without, so we have to be aware of their arising and disbanding. Once we're aware in this way, perceptions will no longer function as a cause of suffering. In other words, they won't give rise to any further thought-formations. The mind will be aware in itself and able to extinguish these things in itself.

So we have to stop things at the level of perception. If we don't, thought-formations will fashion things into issues and then cause consciousness to wobble and waver in all sorts of ways. But these are things we can stop and look at, things we can know with every mental moment.... If we aren't yet really acquainted with the arising and disbanding in the mind, we won't be able to let go. We can talk about letting go, but we can't do it because we don't yet know. As soon as anything arises we grab hold of it—even when actually it's already disbanded, but since we don't really see, we don't know....

So I ask that you understand this basic principle. Don't go grasping after this thing or that, or else you'll get yourself all unsettled. The basic theme is within: Look on in, keep knowing on in until you penetrate everything. The mind will then be free from turmoil. Empty. Quiet. Aware. So keep continuous watch of the mind in and of itself, and you'll come to the point where you simply run out of things to say. Everything will stop on its own, grow still on its own, *because the underlying condition that has stopped and is still is already there,* simply that we aren't aware of it yet.

THE PURE PRESENT

June 3, 1964

We have to catch sight of the sensation of knowing when the mind gains knowledge of anything and yet isn't aware of itself, to see how it latches onto things: physical form, feeling, perceptions, thought-formations, and consciousness. We have to probe on in and look on our own. We can't use the teachings we've memorized to catch sight of these things. That won't get us anywhere at all. We may remember, "The body is inconstant," but even though we can say it, we can't see it.

We have to focus on in to see exactly *how* the body is inconstant, to see how it changes. And we have to focus on feelings—pleasant, painful, and neutral—to see how they change. The same holds true with perceptions, thought-formations, and so forth. We have to focus on them, investigate them, contemplate them to see their characteristics *as they actually are.* Even if you can see these things for only a moment, it'll do you a world of good. You'll be able to catch yourself: The things you thought you knew, you didn't really know at all.... This is why the knowledge we gain in the practice has to keep changing through many, many levels. It doesn't stay on just one level.

So even when you're able to know arising and disbanding with every moment right in the present: If your contemplation isn't continuous, it won't be very clear. You have to know how to contemplate the bare sensation of arising and disbanding, simply arising and disbanding, without any labels of "good" or "bad." Just keep with the pure sensation of arising and disbanding. When you do this, other things will come to intrude—but no matter how they intrude, it's still a matter of arising and disbanding, so you can keep your stance with arising and disbanding in this way.

If you start labeling things, they get confusing. All you need to do is keep looking at the right spot: the bare sensation of arising and disbanding. Simply make sure that you really keep watch of it. Whether there's awareness of sights, sounds, smells, tastes, or tactile sensations, just stay with the sensation of arising and disbanding. Don't go labeling the sight, sound, smell, taste, or tactile sensation. If you can keep watch in this way, you're with the pure present—and there won't be any issues.

When you keep watch in this way, you're keeping watch on inconstancy, on change, as it actually occurs—because even the arising and disbanding changes. It's not the same thing arising and disbanding all the time. First this sort of sensation arises and disbands, then that sort arises and disbands. If you keep watch on bare arising and disbanding like this, you're sure to arrive at insight. But if you keep watch with labels—"That's the sound of a cow," "That's the bark of a dog"—you won't be watching the bare sensation of sound, the bare sensation of arising and disbanding. As soon as there's labeling, thought-formations come along with it. Your senses of touch, sight, hearing, and so forth will continue their bare arising and disbanding, but you won't know it. Instead, you'll label everything—sights, sounds, etc.—and then there will be attachments, feelings of pleasure and displeasure, and you won't know the truth.

The truth keeps going along on its own. Sensations keep arising and then disbanding. If we focus right here—at the consciousness of the bare sensation of sights, sounds, smells, tastes, and tactile sensations, then we'll be able to gain insight quickly....

If we know how to observe things in this way, we'll be able to see easily when the mind is provoked by passion or greed, and even more easily when it's provoked by anger. As for delusion, that's something more subtle... something you have to take a great interest in and investigate carefully. You'll come to see all sorts of hidden things—how the mind is covered with many, many layers of film. It's really fascinating. But then that's what insight meditation is for—to open your eyes so that you can know and see, so that you can destroy your delusion and ignorance.

THE DECEITS OF KNOWING

January 29, 1964

You have to find approaches for contemplating and probing at all times so as to catch sight of the flickerings of awareness, to see in what ways it streams out to know things. Be careful to catch sight of it both when its knowing is right and when it's wrong. Don't mix things up, taking wrong knowledge for right, or right knowledge for wrong. This is something extremely important for the practice, this question of right and wrong knowing, for these things can play tricks on you.

When you gain any new insights, don't go getting excited. You can't let yourself get excited by them at all, because it doesn't take long for your insight to change—to change right now, before your very eyes. It's not going to change at some other time or place. It's changing right now. You have to know how to observe, how to acquaint yourself with the deceits of knowledge. *Even when it's correct knowledge, you can't latch onto it.*

Even though we may have standards for judging what sort of knowledge is correct in the course of our practice, don't go latching onto correct knowledge—because correct knowledge is inconstant. It changes. It can turn into false knowledge, or into knowledge that is even more correct. You have to contemplate things very carefully—very, very carefully—so that you won't fall for your knowledge, thinking, "I've gained right insight; I know better than other people," so that you won't start assuming yourself to be special. The moment you assume yourself, your knowledge immediately turns wrong. Even if you don't let things show outwardly, the mere mental event in which the mind labels itself is a form of wrong knowing that obscures the mind from itself in an insidious way.

This is why meditators who neglect to contemplate things, who don't catch sight of the deceits of every form of knowledge—right and wrong, good and bad—tend to get bogged down in their knowledge. The knowledge that deceives them into thinking, "What I know is right," gives rise to strong pride and conceit within them, without their even realizing it.

This is because the defilements are always getting into the act without our realizing it. They're insidious, and in their insidious way they keep getting into the act as a matter of course, for the defilements and mental effluents are still there in our character. Our practice is basically a probing deep inside, from the outer levels of the mind to the inner ones. This is an approach that requires a great deal of subtlety and precision.... *The mind has to use its own mindfulness and discernment to dig everything out of itself, leaving just the mind in and of itself, the body in and of itself, and then keep watch over them.*

The basic challenge in the practice is this one point and nothing else: *this problem of how to look inward so that you see clear through.* If the mind hasn't been trained to look inward, it tends to look outward, simply waiting to receive its objects from outside—and all it gets is the confusion of its sensations going in and out, in and out. And even though this confusion is one aspect of change and inconstancy, we don't see it that way. Instead, we see it as issues, good and bad, pertaining to the self. When this is the case, we're back right where we started, not knowing what's what. This is why the mind's sensations, when it isn't acquainted with itself, are so secretive and hard to perceive. If you want to find out about them by reading a lot of books, you end up piling more defilements onto the mind, making it even more thickly covered than before.

So when you turn to look inward, you shouldn't use concepts and labels to do your looking for you. If you use concepts and labels to do your looking, there will be nothing but concepts arising, changing, and disbanding. Everything will get all concocted into thoughts—and then how will you be able to watch in utter silence? The more you take what you've learned from books to look inside yourself, the less you'll see.

So whatever you've learned, when you come to the practice you have to put all the labels and concepts you've gained from your learning to one side. You have to make yourself an innocent beginner once more. Only then will you be able to penetrate in to read the truths within you. If you carry all the paraphernalia of the concepts and standards you've gained from your learning to gauge things inside you, you can search to your dying day and yet won't meet with any real truths at all. This is why you have to hold to only one theme in your practice. If the mind has lots of themes to concern itself with, it's still just wandering around—wandering around to know this and that, going out of bounds without realizing it and not really wanting to know itself. This is why those with a lot of learning like to teach others, to show off their level of understanding. And this is precisely how the desire to stand out keeps the mind obscured.

Of all the various kinds of deception, *there's none as bad as deceiving yourself.* When you haven't yet really seen the truth, what business do you have making assumptions about yourself, that you've attained this or that sort of knowledge, or that you know enough to teach others correctly? The Buddha is quite critical of teachers of this sort. He calls them "people in vain." Even if you can teach large numbers of people to become arahants, while you yourself haven't tasted the flavor of the Dhamma, the Buddha says that you're a person in vain. So you have to keep examining yourself. If you haven't yet really trained yourself in the things you teach to others, how will you be able to extinguish your own suffering?

Think about this for a moment. Extinguishing suffering, gaining release from suffering: Aren't these subtle matters?

Aren't they completely personal within us? If you question yourself in this way, you'll be on the right track. But even then you have to be careful. If you start taking sides with yourself, the mind will cover itself up with wrong insights and wrong opinions. If you don't observe really carefully, you can get carried off on a tangent—because the awareness with which the mind reads itself and actually sees through itself is something really extraordinary, really worth developing—and it really eliminates suffering and defilement. This is the real, honest truth, not a lot of propaganda or lies. It's something you really have to practice, and then you'll really have to see clearly in this way. When this is the case, how can you *not* want to practice?

If you examine yourself correctly in this way, you'll be able to know what's real. But you have to be careful to examine yourself correctly. If you start latching onto any sense of self, thinking that you're better than other people, then you've failed the examination. No matter how correct your knowledge, you have to keep humble and respectful above all else. You can't let there be any pride or conceit at all, or it will destroy everything.

This is why the awareness that eliminates the sense of self depends more than anything else on your powers of observation—to check and see if there's still anything in your knowledge or opinions that comes from the force of pride in any sense of self.... You have to use the full power of your mindfulness and discernment to cut these things away. It's nothing you can play around at. If you gain a few insights or let go of things a bit, don't go thinking you're anything special. The defilements don't hold a truce with anyone. They keep coming right out as they like. So you have to be circumspect and examine things on all sides. Only then will you be able to benefit in ways that make your defilements and sufferings lighter and lighter.

When we probe in to find the instigator—the mind, or this

property of consciousness—that's when we're on the right track, and our probing will keep getting results, will keep weakening the germs of craving and wiping them out. In whatever way craving streams out, for "being" or "having" in any way at all, we'll be able to catch sight of it every time. To catch hold and examine this "being" and "having" in this way, though, requires a lot of subtlety. If you aren't really mindful and discerning, you won't be able to catch sight of these things at all, because the mind is continually wanting to be and to have. The germs of defilement lie hidden deep in the seed of the mind, in this property of consciousness. Simply to be aware of them skillfully is no mean feat—so we shouldn't even *think* of trying to wipe them out with our mere opinions. We have to keep contemplating, probing on in, until things come together just right, in a single moment, and then it's like reaching the basic level of knowing that exists on its own, with no willing or intention at all.

This is something that requires careful observation: the difference between willed and unwilled knowing. Sometimes there's the intention to look and be aware within, but there come times when there's no intention to look within, and yet knowledge arises on its own. If you don't yet know, look at the intention to look inward: What is it like? What is it looking for? What does it see? This is a basic approach you have to hold to. This is a level you have to work at, and one in which you have to make use of intention—the intention to look inward in this way....But once you reach the basic level of knowing, then as soon as you happen to focus down and look within, the knowledge will occur on its own.

SABBE DHAMMĀ ANATTĀ

July 9, 1971

One night I was sitting in meditation outside in the open air—my back straight as an arrow—firmly determined to make the mind quiet, but even after a long time it wouldn't settle down. So I thought, "I've been working at this for many days now, and yet my mind won't settle down at all. It's time to stop being so determined and to simply be aware of the mind." I started to take my hands and feet out of the meditation posture, but at the moment I had unfolded one leg but had yet to unfold the other, I could see that my mind was like a pendulum swinging more and more slowly, more and more slowly—until it stopped.

Then there arose an awareness that was sustained by itself. Slowly I put my legs and hands back into position. At the same time, the mind was in a state of awareness absolutely and solidly still, seeing clearly into the elementary phenomena of existence as they arose and disbanded, changing in line with their nature—and also seeing a separate condition inside, with no arising, disbanding, or changing, a condition beyond birth and death: something very difficult to put clearly into words, because it was a realization of the elementary phenomena of nature, completely internal and individual.

After a while I slowly got up and lay down to rest. This state of mind remained there as a stillness that sustained itself deep down inside. Eventually the mind came out of this state and gradually returned to normal.

From this I was able to observe how practice consisting of nothing but fierce desire simply upsets the mind and keeps it from being still. But when one's awareness of the mind is just right, an inner awareness will arise naturally of its own accord. Because of this clear inner awareness, I was able to continue knowing the facts of what's true and false, right and wrong, from that point on, and it enabled me to know that the moment when the mind let go of everything was a clear awareness of the elementary phenomena of nature, because it was an awareness that knew within and saw within of its own accord—not something you can know or see by wanting.

For this reason the Buddha's teaching, *"Sabbe dhammā anattā*—All phenomena are not-self,"* tells us not to latch onto *any* of the phenomena of nature, whether conditioned or unconditioned. From that point on I was able to understand things and let go of attachments step by step.

GOING OUT COLD

May 26, 1964

It's important to realize how to focus on events in order to get special benefits from your practice. You have to focus so as to observe and contemplate, not simply to make the mind still. Focus on how things arise, how they disband. Make your focus subtle and deep.

When you're aware of the characteristics of your sensations, then—if it's a physical sensation—contemplate that physical sensation. There will have to be a feeling of stress. Once there's a feeling of stress, how will you be aware of it simply as a feeling so that it won't lead to anything further? Once you can be aware of it simply as a feeling, it stops right there without producing any taste in terms of a desire for anything. The mind will disengage right there—right there at the feeling. If you don't focus on it in this way, craving will arise on top of the feeling—craving to attain ease and be rid of the stress and pain. If you don't focus on the feeling in the proper way right from the start, craving will arise before you're aware of it, and if you then try to let go of it, it'll be very tiring....

The way in which preoccupations take shape, the sensations of the mind as it's aware of things coming with every moment, the way these things change and disband: These are all things you have to focus on to see clearly. This is why we make the mind disengaged. We don't disengage it so that it doesn't know or amount to anything. That's not the kind of disengagement we want. The more the mind is truly disengaged, the more it sees clearly into the characteristics of the arising and disbanding within itself. All I ask is that you observe things carefully, that your awareness be all-around at all times. Work at this as much as you can. If you can keep this sort of awareness going, you'll find that the mind or consciousness under the supervision of mindfulness and discernment in this way is different from—the direct opposite of— unsupervised consciousness. It will be the opposite sort of thing continually.

If you keep the mind well supervised so that it's sensitive in the proper way, it will yield enormous benefits, not just small ones. If you don't make it properly sensitive and aware, what can you expect to gain from it?

When we say that we gain from the practice, we're not talking about anything else: We're talking about gaining disengagement. Freedom. Emptiness. Before, the mind was embroiled. Defilement and craving attacked and robbed it, leaving it completely entangled. Now it's disengaged, freed from the defilements that used to gang up to burn it. Its desires for this or that thing, its concocting of this or that thought, have all fallen away. So now it's empty and disengaged. It can be empty in this way right before your very eyes. Try to see it right now, before your eyes, right now as I'm speaking and you're listening. Probe on in so as to know.

If you can be constantly aware in this way, you're following in the footsteps or taking within you the quality called *"buddho,"* which means one who knows, who is awake, who has blossomed in the Dhamma. Even if you haven't fully blossomed—if you've blossomed only to the extent of disengaging from the blatant levels of craving and defilement—you still benefit a great deal, for when the mind really knows the defilements and can let them go, it feels cool and refreshed in and of itself. This is the exact opposite of the defilements that, as soon as they arise, make us burn and smoulder inside. If we don't have the mindfulness and discernment to help us know, the defilements will burn us. But as soon as mindfulness and discernment know, the fires go out—and they go out cold.

Observe how the defilements arise and take shape—they also disband in quick succession, but when they disband on their own in this way, go out on their own in this way, they go out hot. If we have mindfulness and discernment watching over them, they go out cold. Look so that you can see what the true knowledge of mindfulness and discernment is like: It goes out; it goes out cold. As for the defilements, even when they arise and disband in line with their nature, they go out hot—hot because we latch onto them, hot because of attachment. When they go out cold, look again—it's because there's no attachment. They've been let go, put out.

This is something really worth looking into: the fact that there's something very special like this in the mind—special in that when it really knows the truth, it isn't attached. It's unentangled, empty, and free. This is how it's special. It can grow empty of greed, anger, and delusion, step after step. It can be empty of desire, empty of mental processes. The important thing is that you really see for yourself that the true nature of the mind is that it can be empty.... This is why I said this morning that *nibbāna* doesn't lie anywhere else. It lies right here, right where things go out and are cool, go out and are cool. It's staring us right in the face.

READING THE HEART

March 15, 1974

The Buddha taught that we are to know with our own hearts and minds. Even though there are many, many words and phrases coined to explain the Dhamma, we need focus only on the things we can know and see, extinguish and let go of, right in each moment of the immediate present—better than taking on a load of other things. Once we can read and comprehend our inner awareness, we'll be struck deep within us that the Buddha awakened to the truth right here in the heart. His truth is truly the language of the heart.

When they translate the Dhamma in all sorts of ways, it becomes something ordinary. But if you keep close and careful watch right at the heart and mind, you'll be able to see clearly, to let go, to put down your burdens. If you don't know right here, your knowledge will send out all sorts of branches, turning into thought-formations with all sorts of meanings in line with conventional labels—and all of them way off the mark.

If you know right at your inner awareness and make it your constant stance, there's nothing at all: no need to take hold of anything, no need to label anything, no need to give anything names. Right where craving arises, right where it disbands: That's where you'll know what *nibbāna* is like.... "*Nibbāna* is simply this disbanding of craving." That's what the Buddha stressed over and over again.

PART II

Breath Meditation Condensed

There are lots of people who are ashamed to talk about their own defilements but who feel no shame at talking about the defilements of others. Those who are willing to report their own diseases—their own defilements—in a straightforward manner are few and far between. As a result, the disease of defilement is hushed up and kept secret, so that we don't realize how serious and widespread it is. We all suffer from it, and yet no one is open about it. No one is really interested in diagnosing his or her own defilements....

We have to find a skillful approach if we hope to wipe out this disease, and we have to be open about it, admitting our defilements from the grossest to the most subtle levels, dissecting them down to their minutest details. Only then will we gain from our practice. If we look at ourselves in a superficial way, we may feel that we're already fine just as we are, that we already know all we need to know. But then when the defilements let loose with full force as anger or delusion, we pretend that nothing is wrong—and this way the defilements become a hidden disease, hard to catch hold of, hard to diagnose....

We have to be strong in fighting off defilements, cravings, and illusions of every sort. We have to test our strength against them and bring them under our power. If we can bring them under our power, we can ride on their backs. If we can't, they'll have to ride on *our* backs, making us do their work,

51

pulling us around by the nose, making us want, wearing us out in all sorts of ways.

So are we still beasts of burden? Are we beasts of burden because defilement and craving are riding on our backs? Have they put a ring through our noses? When you get to the point where you've had enough, you have to stop—stop and watch the defilements to see how they come into being, what they want, what they eat, what they find delicious. Make it your sport—watching the defilements and making them starve, like a person giving up an addiction.... See if it gets the defilements upset. Do they hunger to the point where they're salivating? Then don't let them eat. No matter what, don't let them eat what they're addicted to. After all, there are plenty of other things to eat. You have to be hard on them—hard on your "self"—like this.... "Hungry? Well go ahead and be hungry! You're going to die? Fine! Go ahead and die!" If you can take this attitude, you'll be able to win out over all sorts of addictions, all sorts of defilements—because you're not pandering to desire, you're not nourishing the desire that exists for the sake of finding flavor in physical things. It's time you stopped, time you gave up feeding these things. If they're going to waste away and die, let them die. After all, why should you keep them fat and well fed?

No matter what, you have to keep putting the heat on your cravings and defilements until they wither and waste away. Don't let them raise their heads. Keep them under your thumb. This is the sort of straightforward practice you have to follow. If you're steadfast, if you put up a persistent fight until they're all burned away, then there's no other victory that can come anywhere near, no other victory that's anywhere near a match for victory over the cravings and defilements in your own heart.

This is why the Buddha taught us to put the heat on the defilements in all our activities—sitting, standing, walking, and lying down. If we don't do this, *they'll* burn *us* in all our activities....

If you consider things carefully, you'll see that the Buddha's teachings are all exactly right, both in how they tell us to examine the diseases of defilement and in how they tell us to let go, destroy, and extinguish defilement. All the steps are there, so we needn't go study anywhere else. Every point in his doctrine and discipline shows us the way, so we needn't wonder how we can go about examining and doing away with these diseases. This becomes mysterious and hard to know only if you study his teachings without applying them to doing away with your own defilements. People don't like to talk about their own defilements, so they end up completely ignorant. They grow old and die without knowing a thing about their own defilements at all.

When we start to practice, when we come to comprehend how the defilements burn our own hearts, that's when we gradually come to know ourselves. To understand suffering and defilement and learn how to extinguish defilement gives us space to breathe....

To learn how to put out the fires of defilement, how to destroy them, means we have tools. We can be confident in ourselves—no doubts, no straying off into other paths of practice, because we're sure to see that practicing in this way, contemplating inconstancy, stress, and not-selfness in this way at all times, really gets rid of our defilements.

The same holds true with virtue, concentration, and discernment. They're our tools—and we need a full set. We need the discernment that comes with right view and the virtue that comes with self-discipline. Virtue is very important. Virtue and discernment are like our right and left hands. If one of our hands is dirty, it can't wash itself. You need to use both hands to keep both hands washed and clean. Thus wherever there's virtue, you have to have discernment. Wherever there's discernment, you have to have virtue. Discernment is what enables you to know; virtue is what enables you to let go, to relinquish, to destroy your addictions. Virtue isn't just a matter of the five or eight precepts, you know. It has to deal with the finest details. Whatever your discernment sees as a cause of suffering, you have to stop, you have to let go.

Virtue can get very subtle and precise. Letting go, giving up, renouncing, abstaining, cutting away, and destroying: All of these things are an affair of virtue. This is why virtue and discernment have to go together, just as our right and left hands have to help each other. They help each other wash away defilement. That's when your mind can become centered, bright, and clear. These things show their benefits right at the mind. If we don't have these tools, it's as if we had no hands or feet: We wouldn't be able to get anywhere at all. We have to use our tools—virtue and discernment—to destroy defilement. That's when our minds will benefit....

This is why the Buddha taught us to keep training in virtue, concentration, and discernment. We have to keep fit in training these things. If we don't keep up the training as we should, our tools for extinguishing suffering and defilement won't be sharp, won't be of much use. They won't be a match for the defilements. The defilements have monstrous powers for burning the mind in the twinkling of an eye. Say that the mind is quiet and neutral: The slightest sensory contact can set things burning in an instant by making us pleased or displeased. Why?

Sensory contact is our measuring stick for seeing how firm or weak our mindfulness is. Most of the time it stirs things up. As soon as there's contact by way of the ear or eye, the defilements are very quick. When this is the case, how can we keep things under control? How are we going to gain control over our eyes? How are be going to gain control over our ears, nose, tongue, body, and mind? How can we get mindfulness and discernment in charge of these things? This is a matter of practice, pure and simple ... our own affair, something by which we can test ourselves, to see why defilements flare up so quickly when sensory contact takes place.

Say, for instance, that we hear a person criticizing someone else. We can listen and not get upset. But say that the
thought occurs to us, "She's actually criticizing *me*." As soon
as we conjure up this "me," we're immediately angry and
displeased. If we concoct very much of this "me," we can get
very upset. Just this fact alone should enable us to observe
that as soon as our "self" gets involved, we suffer immediately. This is how it happens. If no sense of self comes out to
get involved, we can remain calm and indifferent. When they
criticize other people, we can stay indifferent; but as soon as
we conclude that they're criticizing us, our "self" appears and
immediately gets involved—and we immediately burn with
defilement. Why?

You have to pay close attention to this. As soon as your
"self" arises, suffering arises in the very same instant. The
same holds true even if you're just thinking. The "self" you
think up spreads out into all sorts of issues. The mind gets
scattered all over the place with defilement, craving, and
attachments. It has very little mindfulness and discernment
watching over it, so it gets dragged all over the place by craving and defilement.

And yet we don't realize it. We think we're just fine. Is
there anyone among us who realizes that this is what's happening? We're too weighed down, weighed down with our
own delusions. No matter how much the mind is smothered
in the defilement of delusion, we don't realize it, for it keeps
us deaf and blind....

There are no physical tools you can use to detect or cure
this disease of defilement, because it arises only at sensory
contact. There's no substance to it. It's like a match in a match-
box. As long as the match doesn't come into contact with the
friction strip on the side of the box, it won't give rise to fire.
But as soon as we strike it against the side of the box, it bursts
into flame. If it goes out right then, all that gets burned is the
matchhead. If it doesn't stop at the matchhead, it'll burn the

matchstick. If it doesn't stop with the matchstick, and meets anything flammable, it can grow into an enormous fire.

When defilement arises in the mind, it starts from the slightest contact. If we can be quick to put it out right there, it's like striking a match that flares up—*chae*—for an instant and then dies down right in the matchhead. The defilement disbands right there. But if we don't put it out the instant it arises, and let it start concocting issues, it's like pouring fuel into a fire.

We have to observe the diseases of defilement in our own minds to see what their symptoms are, why they're so quick to flare up. They can't stand to be disturbed. The minute you disturb them, they flare up into flame. When this is the case, what can we do to prepare ourselves beforehand? How can we stock up on mindfulness before sensory contact strikes?

The way to stock up is to practice meditation, as when we keep the breath in mind. This is what gets our mindfulness prepared, so that we can keep ahead of defilement, so that we can keep it from arising as long as we have our theme of meditation as an inner shelter for the mind.

The mind's outer shelter is the body, which is composed of physical elements, but its inner shelter is the theme of meditation we use to train its mindfulness to be focused and aware. Whatever theme we use, that's the inner shelter for the mind that keeps it from wandering around, concocting thoughts and imaginings. This is why we need a theme of meditation. Don't let the mind chase after its preoccupations the way ordinary people who don't meditate do. Once we have a meditation theme to catch this monkey of a mind so that it becomes less and less willful, day by day, it will gradually calm down, calm down until it can stand firm for long or short periods, depending on how much we train and observe ourselves.

Now, as for how we *do* breath meditation: The texts say to breathe in long and out long—heavy or light—and then to breathe in short and out short, again heavy or light. Those are the first steps of the training. After that we don't have to focus on the length of the in-breath or out-breath. Instead, we simply gather our awareness at any one point of the breath and keep this up until the mind settles down and is still. When the mind is still, you then focus on the stillness of the mind at the same time you're aware of the breath.

At this point you don't focus directly on the breath. You focus on the mind that is still and at normalcy. You focus continuously on the normalcy of the mind at the same time that you're aware of the breath coming in and out, without actually focusing on the breath. You simply stay with the mind, but you watch it with each in-and-out breath. Usually when you are doing physical work and your mind is at normalcy, you can know what you're doing, so why can't you be aware of the breath? After all, it's part of the body.

Some of you are new at this, which is why you don't know how you can focus on the mind at normalcy with each in-and-out breath without focusing directly on the breath itself. What we're doing here is practicing how to be aware of the body and mind, pure and simple, in and of themselves.¸...

Start out by focusing on the breath for about 5, 10, or 20 minutes. Breathe in long and out long, or in short and out short. At the same time, notice the stages in how the mind feels, how it begins to settle down when you have mindfulness watching over the breath. You've got to make a point of observing this, because usually you breathe out of habit, with your attention far away. You don't focus on the breath; you're not really aware of it. This leads you to think that it's hard to stay focused here, but actually it's quite simple. After all, the breath comes in and out on its own, by its very nature. There's nothing at all difficult about breathing. It's not like other themes of meditation. For instance, if you're going to practice recollection of the Buddha, or *buddho*, you have to keep on repeating *buddho, buddho, buddho.*

Actually, if you want, you can repeat *buddho* in the mind with each in-and-out breath, but only in the very beginning stages. You repeat *buddho* to keep the mind from concocting thoughts about other things. Simply by keeping up this repetition you can weaken the mind's tendency to stray, for the mind can take on only one object at a time. This is something you have to observe. The repetition is to prevent the mind from thinking up thoughts and clambering after them.

After you've kept up the repetition—you don't have to count the number of times—the mind will settle down to be aware of the breath with each in-and-out breath. It will begin to be still, neutral, at normalcy.

This is when you focus on the mind instead of the breath. Let go of the breath and focus on the mind—but still be aware of the breath on the side. You don't have to make note of how long or short the breath is. Make note of the mind staying at normalcy with each in-and-out breath. Remember this carefully so that you can put it into practice.

The posture: For focusing on the breath, sitting is a better posture than standing, walking, or lying down, because the sensations that come with the other postures often overcome the sensations of the breath. Walking jolts the body around too much, standing for a long time can make you tired, and if the mind settles down when you're lying down, you tend to fall asleep. With sitting it's possible to stay in one position and keep the mind firmly settled for a long period of time. You can observe the subtleties of the breath and the mind naturally and automatically.

Here I'd like to condense the steps of breath meditation to show how all four of the tetrads mentioned in the texts can be practiced at once. In other words, is it possible to focus on the body, feelings, the mind, and the Dhamma all in one sitting? This is an important question for all of us. You could, if you wanted to, precisely follow all the steps in the texts so as to develop strong powers of mental absorption *(jhāna)*, but it takes a lot of time. It's not appropriate for those of us who are old and have only a little time left.

What we need is a way of gathering our awareness at the breath long enough to make the mind firm, and then go straight to examining how all formations are inconstant, stressful, and not-self, so that we can see the truth of all formations with each in-and-out breath. If you can keep at this continually, without break, your mindfulness will become firm and snug enough for you to give rise to the discernment that will enable you to gain clear knowledge and vision.

So what follows is a guide to the steps in practicing a condensed form of breath meditation.... Give them a try until you find they give rise to knowledge of your own within you. You're sure to give rise to knowledge of your very own.

The first thing to do when you're going to meditate on the breath is to sit straight and keep your mindfulness firm. Breathe in. Breathe out. Make the breath feel open and at ease. Don't tense your hands, your feet, or any of your joints at all. You have to keep your body in a posture that feels appropriate to your breathing. At the beginning, breathe in long and out long, fairly heavily, and gradually the breath will shorten—sometimes heavy and sometimes light. Then breathe in short and out short for about 10 or 15 minutes and then change.

After a while, when you stay focused mindfully on it, the breath will gradually change. Watch it change for as many minutes as you like, then be aware of the whole breath, all of its subtle sensations. This is the third step, the third step of the first tetrad: *sabba-kāya-paṭisamvedi*—focusing on how the breath affects the whole body by watching all the breath sensations in all the various parts of the body, and in particular the sensations related to the in-and-out breath.

From there you focus on the sensation of the breath at any one point. When you do this correctly for a fairly long while, the body—the breath—will gradually grow still. The mind will grow calm. In other words, the breath grows still together with the awareness of the breath. When the subtleties of the breath grow still at the same time that your undistracted awareness settles down, the breath grows even more still. All the sensations in the body gradually grow more and more still. This is the fourth step, the stilling of bodily formations.

As soon as this happens, you begin to be aware of the feelings that arise with the stilling of the body and mind. Whether they are feelings of pleasure or rapture or whatever, they appear clearly enough for you to contemplate them.

The stages through which you have already passed—watching the breath come in and out, long or short—should be enough to make you realize—even though you may not have focused on the idea—that the breath is inconstant. It's continually changing, from in long and out long to in short and out short, from heavy to light and so forth. This should enable you to read the breath, to understand that there's nothing constant to it at all. It changes on its own from one moment to the next.

Once you have realized the inconstancy of the body—in other words, of the breath—you'll be able to see the subtle sensations of pleasure and pain in the realm of feeling. So now you watch feelings, right there in the same place where you've been focusing on the breath. Even though they are feelings that arise from the stillness of the body or mind, they're nevertheless inconstant even in that stillness. They can change. So these changing sensations in the realm of feeling exhibit inconstancy in and of themselves, just like the breath.

When you see change in the body, change in feelings, and change in the mind, this is called *seeing the Dhamma*, i.e. seeing inconstancy. You have to understand this correctly. Practicing the first tetrad of breath meditation contains all four tetrads of breath meditation. In other words, you see the inconstancy of the body and then contemplate feeling. You see the inconstancy of feeling and then contemplate the mind.

The mind, too, is inconstant. This inconstancy of the mind is the Dhamma. To see the Dhamma is to see this inconstancy.

When you see the true nature of all inconstant things, then keep track of that inconstancy at all times, with every in-and-out breath. Keep this up in all your activities to see what happens next.

What happens next is dispassion. Letting go. This is something you have to know for yourself.

This is what condensed breath meditation is like. I call it "condensed" because it contains all the steps at once. You don't have to do one step at a time. Simply focus at one point, the body, and you'll see the inconstancy of the body. When you see the inconstancy of the body, you'll have to see feeling. Feeling will have to show its inconstancy. The mind's sensitivity to feeling, or its thoughts and imaginings, are also inconstant. All of these things keep on changing. This is how you know inconstancy....

If you can become skilled at looking and knowing in this way, you'll be struck with the inconstancy, stressfulness, and not-selfness of your "self," and you'll meet with the genuine Dhamma. The Dhamma that's constantly changing like a burning fire—burning with inconstancy, stress, and not-selfness—is the Dhamma of the impermanence of all formations. But further in, in the mind or in the property of consciousness, is something special, beyond the reach of any kind of fire. There, there's no suffering or stress of any kind at all. This thing that lies "inside": You could say that it lies within the mind, but it isn't really in the mind. It's simply that the contact is there at the mind. There's no way you can really describe it. Only the extinguishing of all defilement will lead you to know it for yourself.

This "something special" within exists by its very nature, but defilements have it surrounded on all sides. All these counterfeit things—the defilements—keep getting in the way and take possession of everything, so that this special nature remains imprisoned inside at all times. Actually, there's nothing in the dimension of time that can be compared with it. There's nothing by which you can label it, but it's something that you can pierce through to see—i.e. by piercing through defilement, craving, and attachment into the state of mind that is pure, bright, and silent. This is the only thing that's important.

But it doesn't have only one level. There are many levels, from the outer bark to the inner bark and on to the sapwood before you reach the heartwood. The genuine Dhamma is like the heartwood, but there's a lot to the mind that isn't heartwood. The roots, the branches and leaves of the tree are more than many, but there's only a little heartwood. The parts that aren't heartwood will gradually decay and disintegrate, but the heartwood doesn't decay. That's one kind of comparison we can make. It's like a tree that dies standing. The leaves fall away, the branches rot away, the bark and sapwood rot away, leaving nothing but the true heartwood. That's one comparison we can make with this thing we call deathless, this property that has no birth, no death, no changing. We can also call it *nibbāna* or the Unconditioned. It's all the same thing.

Now, then, isn't this something worth trying to break through to see?...

PART III

Going Against the Flow

MINDFULNESS LIKE THE PILINGS OF A DAM

November 6, 1970

Discussing the practice is more useful than discussing anything else because it gives rise to insight. If we follow the practice step by step we can *read* ourselves, continually deciphering things within us. As you read yourself through probing and investigating the harm and suffering caused by defilement, craving, and attachment, there will be times when you come to true knowledge, enabling you to grow dispassionate and let go. The mind will then immediately grow still, with none of the mental concoctions that used to have the run of the place through your lack of self-investigation.

The principles of self-investigation are our most important tools. We have to make a concerted effort to master them at all times, with special emphasis on using mindfulness to focus on the mind and bring it to centered concentration. If we don't focus on keeping the mind centered or neutral as its basic stance, it will wander off in various ways in pursuit of preoccupations or sensory contacts, giving rise to turmoil and restlessness. But when we practice restraint over the sensory doors by maintaining continuous mindfulness in the heart, it's like driving in the pilings for a dam. If you've ever seen the pilings for a dam, you'll know that they're driven deep,

deep into the ground so that they're absolutely firm and im-movable. But if you drive them into mud, they're easily swayed by the slightest contact. This should give us an idea of how firm our mindfulness should be in supervising the mind to make it stable, able to withstand sensory contact with-out liking or disliking its objects.

The firmness of your mindfulness is something you have to maintain continuously in your every activity, with every in-and-out breath. The mind will stop being scattered in search for preoccupations. If you don't manage this, then the mind will get stirred up whenever there's sensory contact, like a rudderless ship going wherever the wind and waves will take it. This is why you need mindfulness to guard the mind at every moment. If you can make mindfulness constant, in every activity, the mind will be continuously neutral, ready to probe and investigate for insight.

As a first step in driving in the pilings for our dam—in other words, in making mindfulness firm—we have to focus on neutrality as our basic stance. There's nothing you have to think about. Simply make the mind solid in its neutrality. If you can do this continuously, that's when you'll have a true standard for your investigation, because the mind will have gathered into concentration. But this concentration is some-thing you have to watch over carefully to make sure it's not just oblivious indifference. Make the mind firmly established and centered so that it doesn't get absentminded or distracted as you sit in meditation. Sit straight, maintain steady mind-fulness, and there's nothing else you have to do. Keep the mind firm and neutral, not thinking of anything at all. Make sure this stability stays continuous. When anything pops up, no matter how, keep the mind neutral. For example, if there's a feeling of pleasure or pain, don't focus on the feeling. Sim-ply focus on the stability of the mind—and there will be a sense of neutrality in that stability.

If you're careful not to let the mind get absentminded or

distracted, its concentration will become continuous. For example, if you're going to sit for an hour of meditation, focus on centering the mind like this for the first half hour and then make sure it doesn't wander off anywhere until the hour is up. If you change positions, it's simply an outer change in the body, while the mind is still firmly centered and neutral each moment you're standing, sitting, lying down, or whatever.

Mindfulness is the key factor in all of this, keeping the mind from concocting thoughts or labeling things. *Everything has to stop.* Keep this foundation snug and stable with every in-and-out breath. Then you can relax your focus on the breath, while keeping the mind in the same state of neutrality. Relax your heavy focus so that it feels just right with the breath. The mind will be able to stay in this state for the entire hour, free from any thoughts that might wander off the path. Then keep an eye out to see that no matter what you do or say, the mind stays solidly in its normal state of inward knowing.

If the mind is stable within itself, you're protected on all sides. When sensory contacts come, you stay focused on being aware of your mental stability. Even if there are any momentary slips in your mindfulness, you get right back to the stability of the mind. Other than that, there's nothing you have to do. The mind will let go without you're having to do anything else. The way you used to like this, hate that, turn left here, turn right there, won't be able to happen. The mind will stay neutral, equanimous, just right. If mindfulness lapses, you get right back to your focus, recognizing when the mind is centered and neutral toward its objects and then keeping it that way.

The pilings for the dam of mindfulness have to be driven in so that they're solid and secure with your every activity. Keep working at this no matter what you're doing. If you can train the mind so that stability is its basic stance, it won't get into mischief. It won't cause you any trouble. It won't concoct thoughts. It will be quiet. Once it's quiet and centered, it'll grow more refined and probe in to penetrate within itself, to know its own state of concentration from within.

As for sensory contacts, those are things outside—appearing only to disappear—so it's not interested. This can make cravings disband. Even when we change positions as pains arise in the body, the mind in that moment is stable, focused not on the pains but on its own stability. When you change positions, there will be physical and mental reactions as the circulation improves and pleasant feelings arise in place of the pains, but the mind won't get snagged on either the pleasure or the pain. It will simply stay stable: centered and firm in its neutrality. This stability can easily help you abandon the cravings that lie latent in connection with all feelings. But if you don't keep the mind centered in advance like this, craving will create issues, provoking the mind into a turmoil, wanting to change things so as to get this or that kind of happiness.

If we practice in this way repeatedly, hammering at this point over and over again, it's like driving pilings into the ground. The deeper we can drive them, the more immovable they'll be. That's when you'll be able to withstand sensory contacts. Otherwise, the mind will start boiling over with its thought-concoctions in pursuit of sights, sounds, smells, tastes, and tactile sensations. Sometimes it keeps concocting the same old senseless issues over and over again. This is because the pilings of mindfulness aren't yet firmly in place. The way we've been stumbling through life is due to the fact that we haven't really practiced to the point where mindfulness is continuous enough to make the mind firmly centered and neutral. So we have to make our dam of mindfulness solid and secure.

This centeredness of mind is something we should develop with every activity, with every in-and-out breath. This way we'll be able to see through our illusions, all the way into the truths of inconstancy and not-self. Otherwise, the mind will go straying off here and there like a mischievous monkey—yet even monkeys can be caught and trained to perform tricks. In the same way, the mind is something that can be trained, but if you don't tie it to the post of mindfulness and give it a taste of the stick, it'll be very hard to tame.

When training the mind, you shouldn't force it too much, nor can you simply let it go its habitual ways. You have to test yourself to see what gets results. If you don't get your mindfulness focused, it'll quickly go running out after pre-occupations or easily waver under the impact of its objects. When people let their minds simply drift along with the flow of things, it's because they haven't established mindfulness as a solid stance. When this is the case, they can't stop. They can't grow still. They can't be free. This is why we have to start out by driving in the pilings for our dam so that they're good and solid, keeping the mind stable and centered whether we're sitting, standing, walking, or lying down. This stability will then be able to withstand everything. Your mindfulness will stay with its foundation, just like a monkey tied to a post: It can't run off or get into mischief. It can only circle the post to which its leash is tied.

Keep training the mind until it's tame enough to settle down and investigate things, for if it's still scattered about, it's of no use at all. You have to train it until it's familiar with what inner stability is like, for your own instability and lack of commitment in training it is what allows it to get all entangled with thought-concoctions, with things that arise and then pass away. You have to get it to stop. Why is it so mischievous? Why is it so scattered? Why does it keep wandering off? Get in under control! Get it to stop, to settle down and grow centered!

At this stage you all have practiced enough to gain at least a taste of centered concentration. The next step is to use mindfulness to maintain it in your every activity, so that even if there are any distractions, they last only for a moment and don't turn into long issues. Keep driving in the pilings until they're solid every time there's an impact from external objects, or so that the mental concoctions that go straying out from within are all brought to stillness in every way.

This training isn't really all that hard. The important point is that, whichever of the many meditation subjects you choose, you stay mindful and aware of the mind state that's centered and neutral. If, when the mind goes straying out after objects, you keep bringing it back to its centeredness over and over again, the mind will eventually be able to stay firmly in its stance. In other words, its mindfulness will become constant, ready to probe and investigate, *because when the mind really settles down, it gains the power to read the facts within itself clearly.* If it's not centered, it can jumble everything up to fool you, switching from this issue to that, from this role to that; but if it's centered, it can disband everything—all defilements, cravings, and attachments—on every side.

So what this practice comes down to is how much effort and persistence you put into getting the mind firmly centered. Once it's firm, then when there arise all the sufferings and defilements that would otherwise get it soiled and worked up, it can withstand them just as the pilings of a dam can withstand windstorms without budging. You have to be clearly aware of this state of mind so that you won't go out liking this or hating that. This state will then become your point of departure for probing and investigating so as to gain the insight that sees clearly all the way through—but you have to make sure that this centeredness is continuous. Then you won't have to think about anything. Simply look right in, deeply and subtly.

The important point is that you get rid of absentmindedness and distractions. This in itself gets rid of a lot of delusion and ignorance, and leaves no opening for craving to create any issues that will stir up the mind and set it wandering. This is because we've established our stance in advance. Even if we lose our normal balance a little bit, we get right back to focusing on the stability of our concentration. If we keep at this over and over again, the stability of the mind with its continuous mindfulness will enable us to probe into the truths of inconstancy, stress, and not-self.

In the beginning, though, you don't have to do any probing. It's better simply to focus on the stability of your stance, for if you start probing when the mind isn't really centered and stable, you'll end up scattered. So focus on making centeredness the basic level of the mind and then start probing in deeper and deeper. This will lead to insights that grow more and more telling and profound, bringing the mind to a state of freedom within itself, or to a state where it is no longer hassled by defilement.

This in itself will bring about true mastery over the sense doors. At first, when we started out, we weren't able to exercise any real restraint over the eyes and ears, but once the mind becomes firmly centered, then the eyes, ears, nose, tongue, and body are automatically brought under control. If there's no mindfulness and concentration, you can't keep your eyes under control, because the mind will want to use them to look and to see, it will want to use the ears to listen to all kinds of things. So instead of exercising restraint outside, at the senses, we exercise it inside, right at the mind, making the mind firmly centered and neutral at all times. Regardless of whether you're talking or whatever, the mind's focus stays in place. Once you can do this, you'll regard the objects of the senses as meaningless. You won't have to take issue with things, thinking, "This is good, I like it. This is bad, I don't like it. This is pretty; that's ugly." The same holds true with the sounds you hear. You won't take issue with them. You focus instead on the neutral, uninvolved centeredness of the mind. This is the basic foundation for neutrality.

When you can do this, everything becomes neutral. When the eye sees a form, it's neutral. When the ear hears a sound, it's neutral—the mind is neutral, the sound is neutral, *everything is all neutral*—because we've closed five of the six sense doors and then settled ourselves in neutrality right at the mind. This takes care of everything. Whatever the eye may see, the ear may hear, the nose may smell, the tongue may taste, or the body may touch, the mind doesn't take issue with anything at all. It stays centered, neutral, and impartial. Take just this much and give it a try.

For the next seven days I want you to make a special point of focusing mindfulness right at the mind, for this is the end of the rainy season, the period when the lotus and water lily bloom after the end of the Rains Retreat. In the Buddha's time he would have the senior monks train the new monks throughout the Rains Retreat and then meet with him when the lotuses bloom. I've mentioned this before and I want to mention it again as a way of encouraging you to develop a stable foundation for the mind. If its stability is continuous, then it too will have to bloom—to bloom because it's not burned, disturbed, or provoked by the defilements. So make a special effort during the next seven days to see how you can manage to observe and investigate the centered, neutral state of mind continuously at all times. Of course, if you fall asleep, you fall asleep; but even then, when you lie down to sleep, try to observe how you can keep the mind centered and neutral at all times until you doze off. When you wake up, the movements of the mind will still remain in that centered, neutral state. Give it a try, so that your mind will be able to grow calm and peaceful, disbanding its defilements, cravings, sufferings—everything. Then notice to see whether or not it's beginning to bloom.

The sense of refreshment bathing the mind that comes as part of the peace of mind undisturbed by defilement will arise of its own accord without your having to do anything aside from keeping the mind stable and centered. This is your guarantee: If the mind is really stable in its concentration, the defilements won't be able to burn it or mess with it. In other words, desire won't be able to provoke it. When concentration is stable, the fires of passion, aversion, and delusion won't be able to burn it. Try to see within yourself how the stability of the mind can withstand these things, disbanding the stress, putting out the flames. But you'll have to be earnest in practicing, in making an effort to keep mindfulness truly continuous. This isn't something to play at. You can't let yourself be weak, for if you're weak you won't be able to withstand anything. You'll simply follow the provocations of defilement and craving.

The practice is a matter of stopping so that the mind can settle down and stand fast. It's not a matter of getting into mischief, wandering around to look and listen and get involved in issues. Try to keep the mind stable; in all your activities— eating, defecating, whatever—keep the mind centered within. If you know the state of the mind when it's centered, immovable, no longer wavering, no longer weak, then the basic level of the mind will be free and empty—empty of the things that would burn it, empty because there's no attachment. This is what enables you to ferret out the stability of the mind at every moment. It protects you from all sorts of things. All attachment to self, "me," and "them" is totally wiped out, cut away. The mind is entirely centered. If you can keep this state stable for the entire seven days, it will enable you to reach insight all on your own.

So I ask each of you to see whether or not you'll be able to make it all the way. Check to see how you're doing each day. And make sure you check things carefully. Don't let yourself be lax, sometimes stable, sometimes not. Get so that the mind is absolutely solid. Don't let yourself be weak. You have to be genuine in what you do if you want to reach the genuine extinguishing of suffering and stress. If you're not genuine, you'll end up letting yourself weaken in the face of the provocation of wanting this or wanting that, doing this or doing

71

that, whatever, in the same way that you've been enslaved to desire, agitated by desire for who knows how long.

Your everyday life is where you can test yourself—so get back to the battlefield! Take a firm stance in neutrality. Then the objects that come into contact with the mind will be neutral; the mind itself will feel centered in neutrality. There will be nothing to take issue with in terms of good or bad or whatever. Everything will come to a halt in neutrality—because things in themselves aren't good or bad or self or whatever, simply that the mind has gone and made issues out of them.

So keep looking inward until you see the mind's neutrality and freedom from "self" continuously, and then you'll see how the lotus comes to bloom. If it hasn't bloomed yet, that's because it's withering and dry in the heat of the defilements, cravings, and attachments smoldering in the mind—things we'll have to learn to ferret out until we can disband them. If we don't, the lotus will wither away, its petals falling to the ground and simply rotting there. So make an effort to keep the lotus of the mind stable until it blooms. Don't wonder about what will happen as it blooms. Just keep it stable and make sure it isn't burned by the defilements.

THE BATTLE WITHIN

November 13, 1970

From what I've seen of your reports on your special development of mindfulness to read the facts within yourselves, some of you have really benefited in terms of penetrating in to read what's going on inside, and you've come out with correct understanding. So now I'd like to give you a further piece of advice: In developing mindfulness as a foundation for probing in to know the truth within yourself, you have to apply a level of effort and persistence appropriate to the task. This is because, as we all know, the mind is cloaked in defilements and mental effluents. If we don't train it and force it, it'll turn weak and lax. It won't have any strength. You have to make your persistence more and more constant so that your probing and investigating will be able to see all the way through to clear insight.

Clear insight doesn't come from thinking and speculating. It comes from investigating the mind while it's gathered into an adequate level of calm and stability. You look deeply into every aspect of the mind when it's neutral and calm, free from thought-formations or likes and dislikes for its preoccupations. You have to work at maintaining this state and at the same time probe deeply into it, because superficial knowledge isn't true knowledge. As long as you haven't probed deeply into the mind, you don't really know anything. The mind is simply calm on an external level, and your reading of the aspects of the wanderings of the mind under the influence of defilement, craving, and attachment isn't yet clear.

So you have to try to peer into yourself until you reach a level of awareness that can maintain its balance and let you contemplate your way to sharper understanding. If you don't contemplate so as to give rise to true knowledge, your mindfulness will stay just on the surface.

The same principle holds with contemplating the body. You have to probe deeply into the ways in which the body is repulsive and composed of physical elements. This is what it means to *read* the body so as to understand it, so that you can explore yourself in all your activities. This way you prevent your mind from straying off the path and keep it focused on seeing how it can burn away the defilements as they arise— which is very delicate work.

Being uncomplacent, not letting yourself get distracted by outside things, is what will make the practice go smoothly.

It will enable you to examine the germs in the mind in a skillful way so that you can eliminate the subtlest ones: ignorance and delusion. Normally, we aren't fully aware of even the blatant germs, but now that the blatant ones are inactivated because of the mind's solid focus, we can look into the more profound areas to catch sight of the deceits of craving and defilements in whatever way they move into action. We watch them, know them, and are in a position to abandon them as soon as they wander off in search of sights, sounds, smells, and delicious flavors. Whether they're looking for good physical flavors—bodily pleasure—or good mental flavors, we have to know them from all sides, even though they're not easy to know because of all the many desires we feel for physical pleasure. And on top of that, there are the desires for happiness embued with pleasurable feelings, perceptions that carry pleasurable feelings, thought-formations that carry pleasurable feelings, and consciousness that carries pleasurable feelings. All of these are nothing but desires for illusions, for things that deceive us into getting engrossed and distracted. As a result, it isn't easy for us to understand much of anything at all.

These are subtle matters and they all come under the term "sensual craving"—the desire, lust, and love that provoke the mind into wandering out in search of the enjoyment it remembers from past sights, sounds, smells, tastes, and tactile sensations. Even though these things may have happened long ago, our perceptions bring them back to deceive us with ideas of their being good or bad. Once we latch onto them, they make the mind unsettled and defiled.

So it isn't easy to examine and understand all the various germs within the mind. The external things we're able to know and let go of are only the minor players. The important ones have gathered together to take charge in the mind and won't budge no matter how you try to chase them out. They're stubborn and determined to stay in charge. If you take them on when your mindfulness and discernment aren't equal to the fight, you'll end up losing your inner calm.

So you have to make sure that you don't push the practice too much, without at the same time letting it grow too slack. Find the middle way that's just right. While you're practicing in this way, you'll be able to observe what the mind is like when it has mindfulness and discernment in charge, and then you make the effort to *maintain* that state and keep it constant. That's when the mind will have the opportunity to stop and be still, stable and centered for long periods of time until it's used to being that way.

Now, there are some areas where we have to force the mind and be strict with it. If we're weak and lax, there's no way we can succeed, for we've given in to our own wants for so long already. If we keep giving in to them, they'll become even more of a habit. So you have to use force—the force of your will and the force of your mindfulness and discernment. Even if you get to the point where you have to put your life on the line, you've got to be willing. When the time comes for you really to be serious, you've got to hold out until you come out winning. If you don't win, you don't give up. Sometimes you have to make a vow as a way of forcing yourself to overcome your stubborn desires for physical pleasure that tempt you and lead you astray.

If you're weak and settle for whatever pleasure comes in the immediate present, then when desire comes in the immediate present you fall right for it. If you give in to your wants often in this way, it'll become habitual, for defilement is always looking for the chance to tempt you, to incite you. As when we try to give up an addiction to betel, cigarettes, or meat: It's hard to do because craving is always tempting us. "Take just a little," it says. "Just a taste. It doesn't matter." Craving knows how to fool us, the way a fish is fooled into getting caught on a hook by the bait surrounding the hook, screwing up its courage enough to take just a little, and then a little more, and then a little more until it's sure to get snagged. The demons of defilement have us surrounded on all sides. Once we fall for their delicious flavors, we're sure to get snagged on the hook. No matter how much we struggle and squirm, we can't get free.

You have to realize that gaining victory over your enemies—the cravings and defilements in the heart—is no small matter, no casual affair. You can't let yourself be weak or lax, but you also have to gauge your strength, for you have to figure out how to apply your efforts so as to weaken the defilements and cravings that have had the power of demons overwhelming the mind for so long. It's not the case that you have to battle to the brink of death in every area. With some things—such as giving up addictions—you can mount a full-scale campaign and come out winning without killing yourself in the process. But with other things, more subtle and deep, you have to be more perceptive so as to figure out how to overcome them over the long haul, digging up their roots so that they gradually weaken to the point where your mindfulness and discernment can rise above them. If there are any areas where you're still losing out, you have to take stock of your sensitivities to figure out why. Otherwise, you'll keep losing out, for when the defilements really want something, they trample all over your mindfulness and discernment in their determination to get what they're after: "That's what I want. I don't care what anyone says." They really are that stubborn! So it's no small matter, figuring out how to bring them under control. It's like running into an enemy or a wild beast rushing in to devour you. What are you going to do?

When the defilements arise right before your eyes, you have to be wary. Suppose that you're perfectly aware, and all of a sudden they spring up and confront you: What kind of mindfulness and discernment are you going to use to disband them, to realize that, "These are the hordes of Mara, come to burn and eat me! How am I going to get rid of them?" In other words, how are you going to find a skillful way of contemplating them so as to destroy them right then and there?

We have to do this regardless of whether we're being confronted with physical and mental pain or physical and mental pleasure. Actually, pleasure is more treacherous than pain because it's hard to fathom and easy to fall for. As for pain, no one falls for it because it's so uncomfortable. So how are we going to contemplate so as to let go of *both* the pleasure *and* the pain? This is the problem we're faced with at every moment. It's not the case that when we practice we accept only the pleasure and stop when we run into pain. That's not the case at all. We have to learn how to read *both* sides, to see that the pain is inconstant and stressful, and that the pleasure is inconstant and stressful, too. We have to penetrate clear through these things. Otherwise, we'll be deluded by the deceits of the cravings for pleasure, whether it's physical pleasure or whatever. Our every activity—sitting, standing, walking, lying down—is really for the sake of pleasure, isn't it?

This is why there are so many, many ways in which we're deluded with pleasure. Whatever we do, we do for the sake of pleasure without realizing how deeply we've mired ourselves in suffering and stress. When we contemplate inconstancy, stress, and not-selfness, we don't get anywhere in our contemplation because we haven't seen through pleasure. We still think that it's a good thing. We have to probe into the fact that there's no real ease to physical or mental pleasure. It's all stress. When you can see it from this angle, that's when you'll come to understand inconstancy.

Then once the mind isn't focused on wanting pleasure all the time, its stresses and pains will lighten. It will be able to see them as something common and normal, to see that if you try to change the pains to find ease, there's no ease to be found. In this way, you won't be overly concerned with trying to change the pains, for you'll see that there's no pleasure or ease to the aggregates, that they give nothing but stress and pain. As in the Buddha's teachings we chant every day: "Form is stressful, feeling, perception, thought-formations, and consciousness are all stressful." *The problem is that we haven't investigated into the truth of our own form, feelings, perceptions, thought-formations, and consciousness.* Our insight isn't yet penetrating because we haven't looked from the angle of true knowing. And so we get deluded and lost here and there in our search for pleasure, finding nothing but pain and yet mistaking it for pleasure. This shows that we still haven't opened our ears and eyes; we still don't know the truth. Once we do know the truth, though, the mind will be more inclined to grow still and calm than to go wandering off. The reason it goes wandering off is because it's looking for pleasure, but once it realizes there's no real pleasure to be found in that way, it settles down and grows still.

All the cravings that provoke and unsettle the mind come down to nothing but the desire for pleasure. So we have to contemplate so as to see that the aggregates have no pleasure to offer, that they're stressful in line with their nature. They're not us or ours. Take them apart and have a good look at them, starting with the body. Analyze the body down to is elements so that the mind won't keep latching onto it as "me" or "mine." You have to do this over and over again until you really understand.

It's the same as when we chant the passage for *Recollection while Using the Requisites*—food, clothing, shelter, and medicine—every day. We do this so as to gain real understanding. If we don't do this every day, we forget and get deluded into loving and worrying about the body as "my body," "my self." No matter how much we keep latching onto it over and over again, it's not easy for us to realize what we're doing, even though we have the Buddha's teachings available, explaining these things in every way. Or we may have contemplated to some extent, but we haven't seen things clearly. We've seen only vague impressions and then flitted off oblivious with-

out having probed in to see all the way through. This is because the mind isn't firmly centered. It isn't still. It keeps
wandering off to find things to think about and get itself all
agitated. This way it can't really get to know anything at all.
All it knows are a few little perceptions. This is the way it
has been for who knows how many years now. It's as if our
vision has been clouded by spots that we haven't yet removed
from our eyes.

Those who aren't interested in exploring, who don't make
an effort to get to the facts, don't wonder about anything at
all. They're free from doubt, all right, but it's because their
doubts have been smothered by delusion. If we start exploring and contemplating, we'll have to wonder about the things
we don't yet know: "What's this? What does it mean? How
can I get rid of it?" These are questions that lead us to explore. If we don't explore, it's because we don't have any
intelligence. Or we may gain a few little insights, but we let
them pass so that we never explore deeply into the basic principles of the practice. What little we *do* know doesn't go anywhere, doesn't penetrate into the Noble Truths, because our
mindfulness and discernment run out of strength. Our persistence isn't resilient enough, isn't brave enough. We don't
dare look deeply inside ourselves.

*To go by our own estimates of how far is enough in the practice
is to lie to ourselves.* It keeps us from gaining release from suffering and stress. If you happen to come up with a few
insights, don't go bragging about them, or else you'll end up
deceiving yourself in countless ways. Those who really know,
even when they *have* attained the various stages of insight,
are heedful to keep on exploring. They don't get stuck on
this stage or that. Even when their insights are correct they
don't stop right there and start bragging, for that's the way
of a fool.

Intelligent people, even though they see things clearly, always keep an eye out for the enemies lying in wait for them

on the deeper, more subtle levels ahead. They have to keep penetrating further and further in. They have no sense that this or that level is plenty enough—for how can it be enough? The defilements are still burning away, so how can you brag? Even though your knowledge may be true, how can you be complacent when your mind has yet to establish a foundation for itself?

As you investigate with mindfulness and discernment, complacency is the major problem. You can't be complacent in the practice if you want to keep up with the fact that life is ebbing away, ebbing with every moment. And how should you live so that you can be said to be uncomplacent? This is an extremely important question, for if you're not alive to it, then no matter how many days or months you practice meditation or restraint of the senses, it's simply a temporary exercise. When you're done, you get back to your same old turmoil as before.

And watch out for your mouth. You'll have trouble not bragging, for the defilements will provoke you into speaking. They want to speak, they want to brag, they won't let you stay silent.

If you force yourself in the practice without understanding its true aims, you end up deceiving yourself and go around telling people, "I practiced in silence for so many days, so many months." This is deceiving yourself and others as well. The truth of the matter is that you're still a slave to stupidity, obeying the many levels of defilement and craving within yourself without realizing the fact. If someone praises you, you really prick up your ears, wag your tail and, instead of explaining the harm of the defilements and craving you were able to find within yourself, you simply want to brag.

So the practice of the Dhamma isn't something that you can just muddle your way through. It's something you have to do with your intelligence fully alert—for when you contemplate in a circumspect way, you'll see that there's nothing worth getting engrossed in, that everything—both inside and out—is nothing but an illusion. It's like being adrift, alone in the middle of the ocean with no island or shore in sight. Can you afford just to sit back and relax or make a temporary effort and then brag about it? Of course not! As your investigation penetrates within to ever more subtle levels of the mind, you'll have to become more and more calm and reserved, in the same way that people become more and more circumspect as they grow from children to teenagers and into adults. Your mindfulness and discernment have to keep getting more and more mature in order to understand the right and wrong, the true and false, in whatever arises: That's what will enable you to let go and gain release. And that's what will make your life in the true practice of the Dhamma go smoothly. Otherwise, you'll fool yourself into boasting of how many years you practiced meditation and will eventually find yourself worse off than before, with defilement flaring up in a big way. If this is the way you go, you'll end up tumbling head over heels into fire—for when you raise your head in pride, you run into the flames already burning within yourself.

To practice means to use the fire of mindfulness and discernment as a counter-fire to put out the blaze of the defilements, because the heart and mind are burning with defilement, and when we use the fire of mindfulness and discernment to put out the fire of defilement, the mind can cool down. Do this by being increasingly honest with yourself, without leaving an opening for defilement and craving to insinuate their way into control. You have to be alert. Circumspect. Wise to them. Don't fall for them! To fall for whatever rationale they come up with is a sign that your mindfulness and discernment are still weak. Craving and defilement lead you away by the nose, burning you with their fire right before your very eyes, and yet you're still able to open your mouth to brag!

So turn around and take stock of everything within yourself, take stock of every aspect, because right and wrong, true and false, are all within you. You can't go finding them out-side. The damaging things people say about you are nothing compared to the damage caused inside you when defilement burns you and your feeling of "me" and "mine" raises its head.

If you don't honestly come to your senses, there's no way your practice of the Dhamma can gain you release from the great mass of suffering and stress. You may be able to gain a little knowledge and let go of a few things, but the roots of the problem will still lie buried deep down. So you have to dig them out. You can't relax after little bouts of emptiness and equanimity. That won't accomplish anything, because the defilements and mental effluents lie deep in the personality, and so you have to use mindfulness and discernment to pene-trate deep down to make a precise and thorough examina-tion. Only then will you get results. Otherwise, if you stay only on the blatant level, you can practice until your body lies rotting in its coffin, but you won't have changed any of your basic habits.

Those who are scrupulous by nature, who know how to contemplate their own flaws, will keep on the alert for any signs of pride within themselves. They'll try to control and destroy conceit on every side and won't allow it to swell. The methods we need to use in the practice for examining and destroying the germs within the mind aren't easy to master. For those who don't contemplate themselves thoroughly, the practice may actually only increase their pride, their brag-ging, their desire to go teaching others. But if we turn within and discern the deceits and conceits of self, a profound feel-ing of disenchantment and dismay arises, causing us to pity ourselves for our own stupidity, for the amount to which we've deluded ourselves all along, and for how much effort we'll still need to put into the practice.

So however great the pain and anguish, however many tears bathe your cheeks, persevere! The practice isn't simply a matter of looking for mental and physical pleasure. "Let tears bathe my cheeks, but I'll keep on with my striving at the holy life as long as I live!" That's the way it has to be! Don't quit at the first small difficulty with the thought, "It's a waste of time. I'd do better to follow my cravings and defilements." You can't think like that! You have to take the exact opposite stance: "When they tempt me to grab this, take a lot of that— I won't! However fantastic the object may be, I won't take the bait." Make a firm declaration! This is the only way to get results. Otherwise, you'll never work yourself free, for the defilements have all sorts of tricks up their sleeves. If you get wise to one trick, they simply change to another, and then another.

If we're not observant to see how much we've been deceived by the defilements in all sorts of ways, we won't come to know the truth within ourselves. Other people may fool us now and then, but the defilements fool us all of the time. We fall for them and follow them hook, line, and sinker. Our trust in the Lord Buddha is nothing compared to our trust in them. We're disciples of the demons of craving, letting them lead us ever deeper into their jungle.

If we don't contemplate to see this for ourselves, we're lost in that jungle charnel ground where the demons keep roasting us to make us squirm with desires and every form of distress. Even though you have come to stay in a place with few disturbances, these demons still manage to tempt and draw you away. Just notice how the saliva flows when you come across anything delicious! *So you have to decide to be either a warrior or a loser.* The practice requires that you do battle with defilements and cravings. Always be on your guard, whatever the approach they take to seduce and deceive you. Other people can't come in to lead you away, but these demons of your own defilements can, because you're willing to trust them, to be their slave. You have to contemplate yourself carefully so that you're no longer enslaved to

83

them and can reach total freedom within yourself. Make an effort to develop your mindfulness and discernment so as to gain clear insight and then let go until suffering and stress disband in every way!

ALL THINGS ARE UNWORTHY OF ATTACHMENT

November 21, 1970

It's very beneficial that we have practiced the Dhamma by contemplating ourselves step by step and have—to some extent—come to know the truth. This is because each person has to find the truth within: the truths of stress, its cause, and the path leading to its disbanding. If we don't know these things, we fall into the same sufferings as the rest of the world. We may have come to live in a Dhamma center, yet if we don't know these truths we don't benefit from staying here. The only way we differ from living at home is that we're observing the precepts. If we don't want to be deluded in our practice, these truths are things we have to know. Otherwise, we get deluded into looking for our fun in the stresses and sufferings offered by the world.

Our practice is to contemplate until we understand stress and its cause, in other words, the defilements that have power and authority in the heart and mind. It's only because we have this practice that we can disband these defilements, that we can disband stress every day and at all times. This is something really marvelous. Those who don't practice don't have a clue, even though they live enveloped by defilements and stress. They simply get led around by the nose into more and more suffering, and yet none of them realize what's going on. If we don't make contact with the Dhamma, if we don't practice, we go through birth and death simply to create *kamma* with one another and to keep whirling around in suffering and stress.

We have to contemplate until we really *see* stress: That's when we'll become uncomplacent and try to disband it or to gain release from it. The practice is thus a matter of struggling to gain victory over stress and suffering with better and better results each time. Whatever mistakes we make in whatever way, we have to try to avoid making them again. And we have to contemplate the harm and suffering caused by the more subtle defilements, cravings, and attachments within us. This is why we have to probe into the deeper, more profound parts of the heart—for if we stay only on the superficial levels of emptiness in the mind, we won't gain any profound knowledge at all.

So we train the mind to be mindful and firmly centered, and to fix its focus on looking within, knowing within. Don't let it get distracted outside. When it focuses within, it will come to know the truth: the truth of stress and of the causes of stress—defilement, craving, and attachment—as they arise. It will see what they're like and how to probe inward to disband them

When all is said and done, the practice comes down to one issue, because it focuses exclusively on one thing: stress together with its cause. This is the central issue in human life— even animals are in the same predicament—but our ignorance deludes us into latching onto all kinds of things. This is because of our misunderstandings or wrong views. If we gain right view, we see things correctly. Whenever we see stress, we see its truth. When we see the cause of stress, we see its truth. We both know and see because we've focused on it. *If you don't focus on stress, you won't know it; but as soon as you focus on it, you will.* It's because the mind hasn't focused here that it wanders out oblivious, chasing after its preoccupations.

When we try to focus the mind down, it struggles and resists because it's used to wandering. But if we keep focusing it again and again, more and more frequently until we get a sense of how to bring it under control, then the task ultimately becomes easier because the mind no longer struggles to chase after its preoccupations as it did before. No matter how much it resists when we start training it, eventually we're sure to bring it under our control, getting it to settle down and be still. If it doesn't settle down, you have to contemplate it. You have to show it that you mean business. This is because defilement and craving are very strong. You can't be weak when dealing with them. You have to be brave, to have a fight-to-the-death attitude, and to keep sustaining your efforts. If you're concerned only with finding comfort and pleasure, the day will never come when you'll gain release. You'll have to stay under their power.

Their power envelops everything in our character, making it very difficult for us to find out the truth about ourselves. What we do know is just a smattering, and so we play truant, abandoning the task, and end up seeing that the practice of the Dhamma isn't really important. Thus we don't bother to be strict with ourselves, and instead involve ourselves in all kinds of things, for that's the path the defilements keep pointing out to us. We grope along weakly, making it harder and harder to see stress clearly because we keep giving in to the defilements and taking their bait. When they complain about the slightest discomfort, we quickly pander to them and take the bait again. It's because we're so addicted to the bait that we don't appreciate either the power of craving—as it wanders out after sights, sounds, smells, tastes, etc.—or the harm it causes in making us scattered and restless, unable to stay still and contemplate ourselves. It's always finding things for us to do, to think about, making ourselves suffer, and yet we remain blind to the fact.

Now that we've come to practice the Dhamma, we begin

to have a sense of what's going on. For this reason, whoever practices without being complacent will find that defilement and stress will have to grow lighter and lighter, step by step. The areas where we used to be defeated, we now come out victorious. Where we used to be burned by the defilements, we now have the mindfulness and discernment to burn *them* instead. Only when we stop groping around and really come to our senses will we realize the benefits of the Dhamma, the importance of the practice. Then there is no way that we can abandon the practice, for something inside us keeps forcing us to stay with it. We've seen that if we don't practice to disband defilement and stress, the stress of the defilements will keep piling up. This is why we have to stay with the practice to our last breath.

You have to be firm in not letting yourself be weak and easily led astray. Those who are mindful and discerning will naturally act it this way; those who aren't will keep on following their defilements, ending up back where they were when they hadn't yet started practicing to gain release from stress. They may keep on practicing, but it's hard to tell what they're practicing for—mostly for more stress. This shows that they're still groping around—and when they grope around in this way, they start criticizing the practice as useless and bad.

When people submit readily to defilement and craving, there's no way they can practice, for if you're going to practice, there are a lot of things you have to struggle with and endure. It's like paddling a boat against the stream—you have to use strength if you want to make any headway. It's not easy to go against the stream of the defilements, because they are always ready to pull you down to a lower level. If you aren't mindful and discerning, if you don't use the Lord Buddha's Dhamma to examine yourself, your strength will fail you, for if you have only a little mindfulness and discernment in the face of a lot of defilements, they'll make you vacillate. And if you're living with sweet-talking sycophants, you'll go even further off the path, involved with all sorts of things and oblivious to the practice.

To practice the Dhamma, then, is to go *against* the flow, to go upstream against suffering and stress, because suffering and stress are the main problems. If you don't really contemplate stress, your practice will go nowhere. Stress is where you start, and then you try to trace out its root cause. You have to use your discernment to track down exactly where stress originates, for stress is a result. Once you see the result, you have to track down the cause. Those who are mindful and discerning are never complacent. Whenever stress arises they're sure to search out its causes so that they can eliminate them. This sort of investigation can proceed on many levels, from the coarse to the refined, and requires that you seek advice so that you don't stumble. Otherwise, you may think you can figure it all out in your head—which won't work at all!

The basic Dhamma principles that the Lord Buddha proclaimed for us to use in our contemplation are many, but there's no need to learn them all. Just focusing on some of the more important ones, such as the five aggregates or name and form, will be very useful. But you need to keep making a thorough, all-round examination, not just an occasional probe, so that a feeling of dispassion and disengagement arises and loosens the grip of desire. Use mindfulness to keep constant and close supervision over the senses, and that mindfulness will come to be more present than your tendency to drift off elsewhere. Regardless of what you're doing, saying, or thinking, be on the lookout for whatever will make you slip, for if you're tenacious in sustaining mindfulness, that's how all your stresses and sufferings can be disbanded.

So keep at this. If you fall down a hundred times, get back up a hundred times and resume your stance. The reason mindfulness and discernment are slow to develop is because you're not really sensitive to yourself. The greater your sensitivity, the stronger your mindfulness and discernment will become. As the Lord Buddha said, *"Bhāvitā bahulīkatā"*—which means, "Develop and maximize"—i.e. make the most of your mindfulness.

The way your practice has developed through contemplating and supervising the mind throughout your daily life has already shown its rewards to some extent, so keep stepping up your efforts. Don't let yourself grow weak or lax. You've finally got this opportunity: Can you afford to be complacent? Your life is steadily ebbing away, so you have to compensate by building up more and more mindfulness and discernment until you become mature in the Dhamma. Otherwise, your defilements will remain many and your discernment crude. The older you grow, the more you have to watch out—for we know what happens to old people everywhere.

So seize the moment to develop the faculties of conviction, persistence, mindfulness, concentration, and discernment in a balanced way. Keep contemplating and probing, and you'll protect yourself from wandering out after the world. No matter who tempts you to go with them, you can be sure within yourself that you won't go following them because you no longer have to go believing anyone else or hoping for the baits of the world—*because the baits of the world are poison. The Dhamma has to be the refuge and light of your life.* Once you have this degree of conviction in yourself, you can't help but stride forward without slipping back; but if you waver and wander, unsure of whether or not to keep practicing the Dhamma, watch out: You're sure to get pulled over the cliff and into the pit of fire.

If you aren't free within yourself, you get pulled at from all sides because the world is full of things that keep pulling at you. But those who have the intelligence not to be gullible will see the stress and harm of those things distinctly for themselves. For this reason they're not headed for anything low;

they won't have to keep suffering in the world. They feel dispassion. They lose their taste for all the various baits and lures the world has to offer.

The practice of the Dhamma is what allows us to shake off whatever attractive things used to delude us into holding on. Realize that it won't be long before we die—we won't be here much longer!—so even if anyone offers us incredible wealth, why should we want it? Who could really own it? Who could really control it?

If you can read yourself in this matter, you come to a feeling of dispassion. Disenchantment. You lose your taste for all the lures of the world. You no longer hold them in esteem. If you make use of them, it's for the sake of the benefits they give in terms of the Dhamma, but your disenchantment stays continuous. Even the name and form you've been regarding as "me" and "mine" have been wearing down and falling apart continually. As for the defilements, they're still lying in wait to burn you. So how can you afford to be oblivious? First there's the suffering and stress of the five aggregates, and on top of that there's the suffering and stress caused by defilement, craving, and attachment, stabbing you, slapping you, beating you.

The more you practice and contemplate, the more you become sensitive to this on deeper and deeper levels, and your interest in blatant things outside—good and bad people, good and bad things—gets swept away. You don't have to concern yourself with them, for you're concerned solely with penetrating yourself within, destroying your pride and conceit. Outside affairs aren't important. What's important is how clearly you can see the truth inside until the brightness appears.

The brightness that comes from seeing the truth isn't at all like the light we see outside. Once you really know it, you see that it's indescribable, for it's something entirely personal. It cleans everything out of the heart and mind in line with the strength of our mindfulness and discernment. It's what sweeps and cleans and clears and lets go and disbands things inside. But if we don't have mindfulness and discernment as our means of knowing, contemplating, and letting go, everything inside is dark on all sides. And not only dark, but also full of fire whose poisonous fuel keeps burning away. What could be more terrifying than the fuel burning inside us? Even though it's invisible, it flares up every time there's sensory contact.

The bombs they drop on people to wipe them all out aren't really all that dangerous, for you can die only once per lifetime. But the three bombs of passion, aversion, and delusion keep ripping the heart apart countless times. Normally we don't realize how serious the damage is, but when we come to practice the Dhamma we can take stock of the situation, seeing what it's like when sensory contact comes, at what moments the burning heat of defilement and craving arises, and why they're all so very quick.

When you contemplate how to disband suffering and defilement, you need the proper tools and have to make the effort without being complacent. The fact that we've come to practice out here without any involvements or worldly responsibilities helps speed up the practice. It's extremely beneficial in helping us to examine our inner diseases in detail and to disband suffering and stress continually in line with our mindfulness and discernment. Our burdens grow lighter and we come to realize how much our practice of the Dhamma is progressing in the direction of the cessation of suffering.

Those who don't have the time to come and rest here or to really stop, get carried away with all kinds of distractions. They may say, "I can practice anywhere," but it's just words. The fact of the matter is that their practice is to follow the defilements until their heads are spinning, and yet they can still boast that they can practice anywhere! Their mouths are not in line with their minds, and their minds—burned and beaten by defilement, craving, and attachment—don't realize their situation. They're like worms that live in filth and are happy to stay and die right there in the filth.

People with any mindfulness and discernment feel disgust at the filth of the defilements in the mind. The more they practice, the more sensitive they become, the more their revulsion grows. Before, when our mindfulness and discernment were still crude, we didn't feel this at all. We were happy to play around in the filth within ourselves. But now that we've come to practice, to contemplate from the blatant to the more subtle levels, we sense more and more how disgusting the filth really is. There's nothing to it that's worth falling for at all, because it's all inconstancy, stress, and not-self.

So what's there to want out of life? Those who are ignorant say that we're born to gain wealth and be millionaires, but that kind of life is like falling into hell! If you understand the practice of the Dhamma in the Buddha's footsteps, you realize that nothing is worth having, nothing is worth getting involved with, everything has to be let go.

Those who still latch onto the body, feeling, perceptions, thought-formations, and consciousness as self need to contemplate until they see that the body is stressful, feelings are stressful, perceptions are stressful, thought-formations are stressful, consciousness is stressful—in short, name is stressful and so is form, or in even plainer terms, the body is stressful and so is the mind. *You have to focus on stress.* Once you see it thoroughly, from the blatant to the subtle levels, you'll be able to rise above pleasure and pain because you've let them go. But if you have yet to fully understand stress, you'll still yearn for pleasure—and the more you yearn, the more you suffer.

This holds too for the pleasure that comes when the mind is tranquil. If you let yourself get stuck on it, you're like a person addicted to a drug: Once there's the desire, you take the drug and think yourself happy. But as for how much suffering the repeated desire causes, you don't have the intelligence to see it. All you see is that if you take the drug whenever you want, you're okay.

When people can't shake off their addictions, this is why. They get stuck on the sense of pleasure that comes when they take the drug. They're ingesting sensuality and they keep on wanting more, for only when they ingest more will their hunger subside. But soon it comes back again, so they'll want still more. They keep on ingesting sensuality, stirring up the mind, but don't see that there's any harm or suffering involved. Instead, they say they're happy. When the longing gets really intense, it feels really good to satisfy it. That's what they say. People who have heavy defilements and crude discernment don't see that desire and longing are suffering, and so they don't know how to do away with them. As soon as they take what they want, the desire goes away. Then it comes back again, so they take some more. It comes back again and they take still more—over and over like this, so blind that they don't realize anything at all.

People of intelligence, though, contemplate: "Why is there desire and why do I have to satisfy it? And when it comes back, why do I have to keep satisfying it over and over again?" *Once they realize that the desire in and of itself is what they have to attack,* that by disbanding this one thing they won't feel any disturbance and will never have to suffer from desire again, *that's when they really can gain release from suffering and stress.* But for the most part we don't see things from this angle because we still take our pleasure in consuming things. This is why it's hard for us to practice to abandon desire. All we know is how to feed on the bait, so we don't dare try giving it up—as when people who are addicted to meat-eating are afraid to become vegetarians. Why? Because they're still attached to flavor, still slaves to desire.

If you can't let go of even these blatant things, how can you ever hope to abandon the damp and fermenting desires within you that are so much harder to detect? You still take the most blatant baits. When desire whispers and pleads with you, there you go—pandering to it as quickly as possible. You don't notice how much this tires you out, don't realize that this is the source of the most vicious sufferings that deceive all living beings into falling under its power. Even though the Buddha's teachings reveal the easiest way to use our discernment to contemplate cause and effect in this area, we don't make the effort to contemplate and instead keep swallowing the bait. We get our pleasure and that's all we want, going with the flow of defilement and craving.

Our practice here is to go *against* the flow of every sort of desire and wandering of the mind. It means self-restraint and training in many, many areas: as, for instance, when sights, sounds, smells, tastes, tactile sensations arise and deceive us into liking something and then, a moment later, tiring of it and wanting something else. We get so thoroughly deceived that we end up running frantically all over the place.

The virulent diseases in the mind are more than many. If you don't know how to deal with them, you'll remain under Māra's power. Those who have truly seen stress and suffering will be willing to put their lives on the line in their effort to work free, in the same way the Buddha was willing to put his life on the line in order to gain freedom from suffering and release from the world. He wasn't out after personal comfort at all. Each Buddha-to-be has had to undergo suffering in the world for his own sake and that of others. Each has had to relinquish all of his vast wealth instead of using it for his comfort. So the practice is one of struggle and endurance. Whoever struggles and endures will gain victory—and no other victory can match it. *Gaining control over the defilements is the ultimate victory.* Whatever you contemplate, you can let go: That's the ultimate victory.

So please keep at the effort. You can't let yourself relax after each little victory. The more you keep being victorious, the stronger, more daring, and more resilient your mindfulness and discernment will become in every area, examining everything regardless of whether it comes in by way of the eyes, ears, nose, tongue, body, or mind.

The more you examine yourself, the sharper your mindfulness and discernment will become, understanding how to disband things and let them go. As soon as there's attachment, you'll see the suffering and stress—just as when you touch fire, feel the heat, and immediately let go. This is why the practice of the Dhamma is of supreme worth. It's not just a game you play around with—for the defilements have a great deal of power that's hard to overcome. But if you make the effort to overcome them, they'll weaken as mindfulness and discernment grow stronger. This is when you can say that you're making progress in the Dhamma: when you can disband your own suffering and stress.

So try to go all the way while you still have the breath to breathe. The Buddha said, "Make an effort to attain the as-yet-unattained, reach the as-yet-unreached, realize the as-yet-unrealized." He didn't want us to be weak and vacillating, always making excuses for ourselves, because now that we've ordained we've already made an important sacrifice. In the Buddha's time, no matter where the monks and nuns came from—from royal, wealthy, or ordinary backgrounds—once they had left their homes they cut their family ties and entered the Lord Buddha's lineage without ever returning. To return to the home life, he said, was to become a person of no worth. His only concern was to keep pulling people out, pulling them out of suffering and stress. If we want to escape, we have to follow his example, cutting away worry and concern for our family and relatives by entering his lineage. To live and practice under his discipline is truly the supreme refuge, the supreme way.

Those who follow the principles of the Dhamma-Vinaya—even though they may have managed only an occasional taste of its peace without yet reaching the paths and their fruitions—

pledge their lives to the Buddha, Dhamma, and Sangha. They realize that nothing else they can reach will lead to freedom from suffering, but if they reach this one refuge, they'll gain total release. Those whose mindfulness and discernment are deep, far-seeing, and meticulous will cross over to the further shore. They've lived long enough on this shore and have had all the suffering they can bear. They've circled around in birth and death countless times. So now they realize that they have to go to the further shore and so they make a relentless effort to let go of their sense of self.

There's nothing distant about the further shore, but to get there you first have to give up your sense of self in the five aggregates by investigating to see them all as stress, to see that none of them are "me" or "mine." Focus on this one theme: not clinging. The Lord Buddha once spoke of the past as below, the future as above, and the present as in the middle. He also said that unskillful qualities are below, skillful qualities above, and neutral ones in the middle. To each of them, he said, "Don't cling to it." Even *nibbāna*, the further shore, shouldn't be clung to. *See how far we're going to be released through not-clinging!* Any of you who can't comprehend that even *nibbāna* isn't to be clung to should consider the standard teaching that tells us not to cling, that we have to let go: "All things are unworthy of attachment." This is the ultimate summary of all that the Buddha taught.

All phenomena, whether compounded or uncompounded, fall under the phrase, *"Sabbe dhammā anattā*—All things are not-self."* They're all unworthy of attachment. This summarizes everything, including our investigation to see the truth of the world and of the Dhamma, to see things clearly with our mindfulness and discernment, penetrating through the compounded to the uncompounded, or through the worldly to the transcendent, all of which has to be done by looking within, not without.

And if we want to see the real essence of the Dhamma, we

have to look deeply, profoundly. Then it's simply a matter of letting go all along the way. We see all the way in and let go of everything. The theme of *not clinging* covers everything from beginning to end. If our practice is to go correctly, it's because we look with mindfulness and discernment to penetrate everything, not getting stuck on any form, feeling, perception, thought-formation, or consciousness at all.

The Buddha taught about how ignorance—not knowing form, delusion with form—leads to craving, the mental act that arises at the mind and agitates it, leading to the *kamma* by which we try to get what we crave. When you understand this, you can practice correctly, for you know that you have to disband the craving. The reason we contemplate the body and mind over and over again is so that we won't feel desire for anything outside, won't get engrossed in anything outside. The more you contemplate, the more things outside seem pitiful and not worth getting engrossed in at all. The reason you were engrossed and excited was because you didn't know. And so you raved about people and things and made a lot of fuss, talking about worldly matters: "This is good, that's bad, she's good, he's bad." The mind got all scattered in worldly affairs—and so how could you examine the diseases within your own mind?

The Buddha answered Mogharāja's question—"In what way does one view the world so that the King of Death does not see one?"—by telling him to see the world as empty, as devoid of self. We have to strip away conventions, such as "person" and "being," and all designations such as elements, aggregates, and sense media. Once we know how to strip away conventions and designations, there's nothing we need to hold onto. What's left is the Deathless. The transcendent. *Nibbāna*. There are many names for it, but they're all one and the same thing. When you strip away all worldly things, what's left is the transcendent. When you strip away all compounded things, what's left is the uncompounded, the true Dhamma.

So consider for yourself whether or not this is worth attaining. If we stay in the world, we have to go through repeated births and deaths in the three levels of existence: sensuality, form, and formlessness. But on that further shore there's no birth, no death. It's beyond the reach of the King of Death. But because we don't know the further shore, we want to keep on being reborn on this shore with its innumerable repeated sufferings.

Once you comprehend suffering and stress, though, there's nowhere else you want to turn: You head straight for the further shore, the shore with no birth or death, the shore where defilement and craving disband once and for all. Your practice thus goes straight to the cessation of suffering and defilement, to clear penetration of the common characteristics of inconstancy, stress, and not-selfness in the aggregates. People with mindfulness and discernment focus their contemplation in the direction of absolute disbanding, for if their disbanding isn't absolute, they'll have to be reborn again in suffering and stress. So keep disbanding attachments, keep letting go, contemplating inconstancy, stress, and not-selfness and relinquishing them. This is the right path for sure.

Isn't this something worth knowing and training for? It's not all that mysterious or far away. It's something that anyone—any man or woman—can realize, something we can all train in. We can develop virtue, can make the mind quiet, and can use our mindfulness and discernment to contemplate. So isn't this really worth practicing?

Stupid people like to say no. They say they can't do it: They can't observe the precepts, can't make the mind quiet. The best thing in life—the practice for release from suffering and stress—and yet they reject it. Instead, they rush around in a turmoil, competing with one another, bragging to one another, and then end up rotting in their coffins. Exactly what is appealing about all that?

We've gone astray for far too long already, our lives almost gone after how many decades. Now we've come here to turn ourselves around. No matter how old you are, the air you breathe isn't just for your convenience and comfort, but for you to learn about suffering and stress. That way you'll be able to disband it. Don't imagine that your family and relatives are essential to you. You are alone. You came alone and you'll go alone. This holds true for each of us. *Only when there's no self to go:* That's when you penetrate to the Dhamma. If there is still a self to be born, then you're stuck in the cycle of suffering and stress. So isn't it worthwhile to strive for release? After all, it's something each of us has to find for himself or herself.

All those who trust in the Lord Buddha will have to follow this way. To trust the defilements is to throw yourself down in the mire—and there who will you be able to brag to, aside from your own sufferings? The knowledge that leads to dispassion and disenchantment is what counts as true knowledge. But if your knowledge leads you to hold on, then you're a disciple of Māra. You still find things very delicious. You may say that you're disenchanted, but the mind isn't disenchanted at all. It still wants to take this, to get that, to stay right here.

If you can keep reading the truth within your own mind, deeper and deeper, you'll be able to go all the way through, wiping out stupidity and delusion each step along the way. Where you used to be deluded, you've now begun to come to your senses. Where you used to brag, you now realize how very stupid you were—and that you'll have to keep on correcting your stupidity.

Reading yourself, contemplating yourself, you see new angles, you gain more precise self-knowledge each step along the way. It's not a question of being expert about things outside. You see how what's inside is really inconstant, really stressful, really not-self. The way you used to fall for things and latch onto them was because of your blindness, because you didn't understand. So who can you blame? Your own stupidity, that's who—because it wanted to brag about how much it knew.

Now you know that you've still got a lot of stupidity left and that you'll have to get rid of it before you die. Every day that you still have breath left to breathe, you'll use it to wipe out your stupidity rather than to get this or be that or to dance around. The ones who dance around are possessed by spirits: the demons of defilement making them crazy and deluded, wanting to get this and be that and dance all over the place. But if you focus your attention in on yourself, then your pride, your conceit, your desires to stand out will shrink out of sight, never daring to show their faces for the rest of your life, for you realize that the more you brag, the more you suffer.

So the essence of the practice is to turn around and focus inside. The more you can wash away these things, the more empty and free the mind will be: This is its own reward. If you connive with your conceits, you'll destroy whatever virtue you have, but if you can drive these demons away, virtuous influences will come and stay with you. If the demons are still there, the virtuous ones won't be able to stay. They can't get along at all. If you let yourself get entangled in turmoil, it's an affair of the demons. If you're empty and free, it's an affair of cleanliness and peace—an affair of the virtuous influences.

So go and check to see how many of these demons you've been able to sweep away. Are they thinning out? When they make an appearance, point them right in the face and call them what they are: demons and devils, come to eat your heart and drink your blood. You've let them eat you before, but now you've finally come to your senses and can drive them away. That will put an end to your troubles, or at least help your sufferings grow lighter. Your sense of self will start to shrivel away. Before, it was big, fat, and powerful, but now its power is gone. Your pride and conceit have grown thin and weak. It's as when a person has been bitten by a rabid dog: They give him a serum made from rabid dogs to drive out the disease. The same holds here: If we can recognize these things, they disband. The mind is then empty and at peace, for this one thing—the theme of not clinging—can disband suffering and stress with every moment.

SIMPLY STOP RIGHT HERE

November 28, 1970

When we contemplate to the point of giving rise to knowledge through genuine mindfulness and discernment, we realize how this is a process of disbanding suffering and defilement. Whenever mindfulness lapses and we latch on to anything, our practice of reading ourselves step by step will enable us to realize the situation easily. This helps us keep the mind under control and does immense good. Still, it's not enough, for the affairs of suffering and defilement are paramount issues buried deep in the character. We thus we have to contemplate and examine things within ourselves.

Looking outside is something we're already used to: Whenever we know things outside, the mind is in turmoil instead of being empty and at peace. This is something we can all be aware of. And this is why we have to maintain the mind in its state of neutrality or mindful centeredness. We then notice from our experience in the practice: What state have we been able to maintain the mind in? Is our mindfulness continuous throughout all our activities? These are things we all have to notice, using our own powers of observation. When the mind deviates from its foundation because of mental fabrications, thinking up all sorts of turmoil for itself as it's used to doing, what can we do to make it settle down and grow still? If it doesn't grow still, it gets involved in nothing but stress: wandering around thinking, imagining, taking on all sorts of things. *That's* stress. You have to keep reading these things at all times, seeing clearly the ways in which they're inconstant, changing, and stressful.

Now, if you understand the nature of arising and passing away by turning inward to watch the arising and passing away within yourself, you realize that it's neither good nor bad nor anything of the sort. It's simply a natural process of arising, persisting, and passing away. Try to see deeply into this, and you'll be sweeping the mind clean, just as when you constantly sweep out your house: If anything then comes to make it dirty, you'll be able to detect it. So with every moment, we have to sweep out whatever arises, persists, and then passes away. Let it all pass away, without latching on or clinging to anything. Try to make the mind aware of this state of unattachment within itself: If it doesn't latch on to anything, doesn't cling to anything, there's no commotion in it. It's empty and at peace.

This state of awareness is *so* worth knowing, for it doesn't require that you know a lot of things at all. You simply have to contemplate so as to see the inconstancy of form, feelings, perceptions, thought-formations, and consciousness. Or you can contemplate whatever preoccupies the mind as it continually changes—arising and passing away—with every moment. This is something you have to contemplate until you really *know* it. Otherwise, you'll fall for your preoccupations in line with the way you label sensory contacts. If you don't fall for sensory contacts arising in the present, you fall for your memories or thought-formations. This is why you have to train the mind to stay firmly centered in neutrality without latching onto anything at all. *If you can maintain this one stance continuously, you'll be sweeping everything out of the mind,* disbanding its suffering and stress in the immediate present with each and every moment.

Everything arises and then passes away, arises and then passes away—everything. Don't grasp hold of anything, thinking that it's good or bad or taking it as your self. Stop all your discursive thinking and mental fabrications. When you can maintain this state of awareness, the mind will calm down on its own, will naturally become empty and free. If any thoughts arise, see that they just come and go, so don't latch onto them. When you can read the aspects of the mind that arise and pass away, there's not much else to do: Just keep watching and letting go within yourself, and no long drawn-out trains of thought about past or future will remain. They all stop right at the arising and passing away.

When you really see the present with its arisings and passings away, there are no great issues. Whatever you think about will all pass away, *but if you can't notice its passing away, you'll grasp at whatever comes up,* and then everything will become a turmoil of ceaseless imaginings. So you have to cut off these connected thought-formations that keep flowing like a stream of water. Establish your mindfulness and, once it's established, simply fix your whole attention on the mind. Then you'll be able to still the flow of thought-formations that had you distracted. You can do this at any time, and the mind will always grow still to become empty, unentangled, unattached. Then keep watch over the normalcy of the mind again and again whenever it gets engrossed and starts spinning out long drawn-out thought-formations. As soon as you're aware, let them stop. As soon as you're aware, let them stop, and things will disband right there. Whatever the issue, disband it immediately. Practice like this until you become skilled at it, and the mind won't get involved in distractions.

It's like driving a car: When you want to stop, just slam on the brakes and you stop immediately. The same principle works with the mind. You'll notice that, no matter when, as soon as there's mindfulness, it stops and grows still. In other words, when mindfulness is firmly centered, then no matter what happens, as soon as you're mindfully aware of it, the mind stops, disengages, and is free. This is a really simple method: stopping as soon as you're mindful. Any other approach is just too slow to cope. This method of examining yourself, knowing yourself, is very worth knowing because anyone can apply it at any time. Even right here while I'm speaking and you're listening, just focus your attention right at the mind as it's normal in the present. This is an excellent way of knowing your own mind.

Before we knew anything about all this, we let the mind go chasing after any thoughts that occurred to it, taking up a new thought as soon as it was finished with an old one, spinning its webs to trap us in all kinds of complications. Whatever meditation techniques we tried weren't really able to stop our distraction. So don't underestimate this method as being too simple. Train yourself to be on top of any objects that make contact or any opinions that intrude on your awareness. When pride and opinions come pouring out, cry, "Stop! Let me finish first!" This method of calling a halt can really still the defilements immediately, even when they're like two people interrupting each other to speak, the conceit or sense of "self" on one side immediately raising objections before the other side has even finished. Or you might say it's like suddenly running into a dangerous beast—a tiger or poisonous snake—with no means of escape. All you can do is simply stop, totally still, and spread thoughts of loving-kindness.

The same holds true here: You simply stop, and that cuts the strength of the defilement or any sense of self that's made a sudden appearance. We have to stop the defilements in their tracks, for if we don't, they'll grow strong and keep intensifying. So we have to stop them right from the first. Resist them right from the first. This way your mindfulness will get used to dealing with them. As soon as you say, "Stop!", things stop immediately. The defilements will grow obedient and won't dare push you around in any way.

If you're going to sit for an hour, make sure that you're mindful right at the mind the whole time. Don't just aim at the pleasure of tranquillity. Sit and watch the sensations within the mind to see how it's centered. Don't concern yourself with any cravings or feelings that arise. Even if pain arises, in whatever way, don't pay it any attention. Keep being mindful of the centered normalcy of the mind at all times. The mind won't stray off to any pleasures or pains, but will let go of them all, seeing the pains as an affair of the aggregates, because the aggregates are inconstant. Feelings are inconstant. The body's inconstant. That's the way they have to be.

When a pleasant feeling arises, the craving that wants pleasure is contented with it and wants to stay with that pleasure as long as possible. But when there's pain, it acts in an entirely opposite way, because pain hurts. When pains arise as we sit for long periods of time, the mind gets agitated because craving pushes for a change. It wants us to adjust things in this way or that. *We have to train ourselves to disband the craving instead.* If pains grow strong in the body, we have to practice staying at equanimity by realizing that they're the pains of the aggregates—and not our pain—until the mind is no longer agitated and can return to a normal state of equanimity.

Even if the equanimity isn't complete, don't worry about it. Simply make sure that the mind doesn't struggle to change the situation. Keep disbanding the struggling, the craving. If the pain is so unbearable that you have to change positions, don't make the change while the mind is really worked up. Keep sitting still, watch how far the pain goes, and change positions only when the right moment comes. Then as you stretch out your leg, make sure that the mind is still centered, still at equanimity. Stay that way for about five minutes, and the fierce pain will go away. But watch out: When a pleasant feeling replaces the pain, the mind will like it. So you have to use mindfulness to keep the mind neutral and at equanimity.

Practice this in all your activities, because the mind tends to get engrossed with pleasant feelings. It can even get engrossed with neutral feelings. So you have to keep your mindfulness firmly established, knowing feelings for what they really are: inconstant and stressful, with no real pleasure to them at all. Contemplate pleasant feelings to see them as nothing but stress. You have to keep doing this at all times. Don't get infatuated with pleasant feelings, for if you do, you fall into more suffering and stress, because craving wants nothing but pleasure even though the aggregates have no pleasure to offer. The physical and mental aggregates are all stressful. If the mind can rise above pleasure, above pain, above feeling, *right there is where it gains release*. Please understand this: It's release from feeling. If the mind hasn't yet gained release from feeling—if it still wants pleasure, is still attached to pleasure and pain—then try to notice the state of mind at the moments when it's neutral toward feeling. That will enable it to gain release from suffering and stress.

So we have to practice a lot with feelings of physical pain and, at the same time, to make an effort to comprehend pleasant feelings as well, for the pleasant feelings connected with the subtle defilements of passion and craving are things we don't really understand. We think that they're true pleasure, which makes us want them. This wanting is craving—and the Buddha tells us to abandon craving and passion for name and form. "Passion" here means wanting to get nothing but pleasure and then becoming entangled in liking or disliking what results. It means that we're entangled in the delicious flavors of feelings, regardless of whether they're physical feelings or mental ones.

We should come to realize that when a feeling of physical pain gets very strong, we *can* handle it by using mindfulness to keep the mind from struggling. Then, even if there's a great deal of physical pain, we can let go. Even though the body may be agitated, the mind isn't agitated along with it. But to do this, you first have to practice separating feelings from the mind while you're still strong and healthy.

As for the feelings that come with desire, if we accumulate them they lead to even greater suffering. So don't think of them as being easeful or comfortable, because that's delusion. You have to keep track of how feelings—no matter what the sort—are all inconstant, stressful, and not-self. If you can let go of feeling, you'll become disenchanted with form, feelings, perceptions, thought-formations, and consciousness that carry feelings of pleasure. But if you don't contemplate these things, you'll stay infatuated with them.

So try noticing when the mind is in this infatuated state. Is it empty and at peace? If it's attached, you'll see that it's dirty and defiled because it's deluded into clinging. As soon as there's pain, it grows all agitated. If the mind is addicted to the three kinds of feeling—pleasant, painful, and neither pleasant nor painful—it has to endure suffering and stress. We have to see the inconstancy, stressfulness, and not-selfness of the body and mind so that we won't cling: We won't cling whether we look outside or inside. We'll be empty—empty because of our lack of attachment. We'll know that the mind isn't suffering from stress. The more deeply we look inside, the more we'll see that the mind is truly empty of attachment.

This is how we gain release from suffering and stress. It's the simplest way to gain release, but if we don't really understand, it's the hardest. Thus you absolutely have to keep working at letting go. The moment the mind latches onto anything, make it let go. And then notice to see that when you tell the mind to let go, it does let go. When you tell it to stop, it stops. When you tell it to be empty, it's really and truly empty.

This method of watching the mind is extremely useful, but we're rarely interested in contemplating to the point of becoming adept and resourceful at disbanding our own sufferings. We practice in a leisurely, casual way, and don't know which points we should correct, where we should disband things, what we should let go of. And so we keep circling around with suffering and attachment.

We have to figure out how to find our opportunity to disband suffering with every moment. We can't just live, sleep, and eat at our ease. We need to find ways to examine and contemplate all things, using our mindfulness and discernment to see their emptiness of "self." Only then will we be able to loosen our attachments. If we don't know with real mindfulness and discernment, our practice won't be able to lead us out of suffering and stress at all.

Every defilement—each one in the list of sixteen—is hard to abandon. Still, they don't arise all sixteen at once, but only one at a time. If you know the features of their arising, you can let them go. The first step is to recognize their faces clearly, because you have to realize that they're burning hot every time they arise. If they have you sad or upset, it's easy to know them. If they have you happy, they're harder to detect. So you first have to learn to recognize the mind at normalcy, keeping your words and deeds at normalcy, too. "Normalcy" here means being free of liking and disliking. It's a question of purity in virtue—just as when we practice restraint of the senses. Normalcy is the basic foundation. If the mind isn't at normalcy—if it likes this or dislikes that—that means your restraint of the senses isn't pure. For instance, when you see a sight with the eye or hear a sound with the ear, you don't get upset as long as no real pains arise, but if you get distracted and absentminded as the pains get more and more earnest, your precepts will suffer, and you'll end up all agitated.

So don't underestimate even the smallest things. Use your mindfulness and discernment to disband things, to destroy them, and to keep working at your investigation. Then, even if serious events happen, you'll be able to let go of them. If your attachments are heavy, you'll be able to let go of them. If they're many, you'll be able to thin them out.

The same holds true with intermediate defilements: the five hindrances. Any liking for sights, sounds, smells, tastes, and tactile sensations is the hindrance of sensual desire. If you don't like what you see, hear, etc., that's the hindrance of ill will. These hindrances of liking and disliking defile the mind, making it agitated and scattered, unable to grow calm. Try observing the mind when it's dominated by the five hindrances to see whether or not it's in a state of suffering. Do you recognize these intermediate defilements when they enshroud your mind?

The hindrance of sensual desire is like a dye that clouds clear water, making it murky—and when the mind is murky, it's suffering. Ill will as a hindrance is irritability and dissatisfaction, and the hindrance of sloth and torpor is a state of drowsiness and lethargy—a condition of refusing to deal with anything at all, burying yourself in sleep and lazy forgetfulness. All the hindrances, including the final pair—restlessness-and-anxiety, and uncertainty—cloak the mind in darkness. This is why you need to be resilient in fighting them off at every moment and in investigating them so that you can weaken and eliminate every form of defilement—from the gross to the middling and on to the subtle—from the mind.

The practice of the Dhamma is very delicate work, requiring that you use all your mindfulness and discernment in probing and comprehending the body and mind. When you look into the body, try to see the truth of how it's inconstant, stressful, and nothing more than physical elements. If you don't contemplate in this way, your practice will simply grope around and won't be able to release you from suffering and stress—for the sufferings caused by the defilements concocting things in the mind are more than many. The mind is full of all kinds of tricks. Sometimes you may gain some insight through mindfulness and discernment—becoming bright, empty, and at peace—only to find the defilements slipping in to spoil things, cloaking the mind in total darkness once more, so that you get distracted and can't know anything clearly.

We each have to find special strategies in reading ourselves so that we don't get lost in distractions. Desire is a big trouble-maker here, and so is distraction. Torpor and lethargy—*all* the hindrances—are enemies blocking your way. The fact that you haven't seen anything all the way through is because these characters are blocking your way and have you sur-rounded. You have to find a way to destroy them using *apt attention,* i.e. a skillful way of making use of the mind. You have to dig down and explore, contemplating to see how these things arise, how they pass away, and what exactly is incon-stant, stressful, and not-self. These are questions you have to keep asking yourself so that the mind will really come to know. When you really know inconstancy, you're sure to let go of defilement, craving, and attachment, or at least be able to weaken and thin them out. It's like having a broom in your hand. Whenever attachment arises, you sweep it away until the mind can no longer grow attached to anything, for there's nothing left for it to be attached to. You've seen that every-thing is inconstant, so what's there to latch onto?

When you're persistent in contemplating to see your incon-stancy, stress, and not-selfness, the mind feels at ease because you've loosened your attachments. This is the marvel of the Dhamma: an ease of body and mind completely free from entanglement in the defilements. It's truly special. Before, the ignorance obscuring the mind caused you to wander about spellbound by sights, sounds, and so forth, so that defilement, craving, and attachment had you under their power. But now, mindfulness and discernment break the spell by showing that there's no self to these things, nothing real to them at all. They simply arise and pass away with every moment. There's not the least little bit of "me" or "mine" to them at all. Once we really know with mindfulness and discernment, we sweep everything clean, leaving nothing but pure Dhamma with no sense of self at all. We see nothing but inconstancy, stress, and not-selfness, with no pleasure or pain.

The Lord Buddha taught, "*Sabbe dhammā anattā*—All things are not-self." Both the compounded and the uncompounded—which is *nibbāna*, the transcendent—are not-self. There's just Dhamma. *This is very important.* There's no sense of self there, but what *is* there, is Dhamma. This isn't the extinction taught by the wrong view of annihilationism; it's the extinction of all attachment to "me" and "mine." All that remains is Deathlessness—the undying Dhamma, the undying property—free from birth, ageing, illness, and death. Everything still remains as it was, it hasn't been annihilated anywhere; the only things annihilated are the defilements together with all suffering and stress. It's called "*suñño*"—empty—because it's empty of the label of self. *This Deathlessness is the true marvel the Buddha discovered and taught to awaken us.*

This is why it's so worth looking in to penetrate clear through the inconstancy, stress, and not-selfness of the five aggregates, for what then remains is the natural Dhamma free from birth, ageing, illness, and death. It's called Unbinding, Emptiness, the Unconditioned: These names all mean the same thing. They're simply conventional designations that also have to be let go so that you can dwell in the aspect of mind devoid of any sense of self.

So the paths, fruitions, and *nibbāna* are not something to hope for in a future life by developing a vast heap of perfections. Some people like to point out that the Lord Buddha had to accumulate so many, many virtues—but what about you? You don't consider how many lives have passed while you still have yet to attain the goal, all because of your stupidity in continually finding excuses for yourself.

The basic principles that the Lord Buddha taught—such as the four foundations of mindfulness, the Four Noble Truths, the three characteristics of inconstancy, stress, and not-selfness—are right here inside you, so probe on in to contemplate them until you know them. Defilement, craving, and attachment are right here inside you, too, so contemplate them until you gain true insight. Then you'll be able to let them go, no longer latching onto them as really being "me" or "mine." This way you'll gain release from suffering and stress within yourself.

Don't keep excusing yourself by relying, for instance, on the miraculous powers of some object or waiting to build up the perfections. Don't think in those terms. Think instead of what the defilements are like right here and now: Is it better to disband them or to fall in with them? If you fall in with them, is there suffering and stress? You have to find out the truth within yourself so as to get rid of your stupidity and delusion in thinking that this bodily frame of suffering is really happiness.

We're all stuck in this delusion because we don't open our eyes. This is why we have to keep discussing these issues, giving advice and digging out the truth so that you'll give rise to the mindfulness and discernment that will enable you to know yourself. The fact that you've begun to see things, to acknowledge the defilements and stress within yourself at least to some extent, is very beneficial. It's better that we talk about these things than about anything else, so that we'll gain knowledge about suffering and its cause, about how to contemplate body, feelings, mind, and mental qualities so as to disband our suffering and stress. This way we can reduce our suffering because we'll be letting go of the defilements that agitate and scorch the mind. Our mindfulness and discernment will gradually be able to eliminate the defilements and cravings from the heart.

This practice of ours, if we really do it and really come to know, will really reduce our sufferings. This will attract others to follow our example. We won't have to advertise, for they'll have to notice. We don't have to brag about what level we've attained or what degrees we've earned. We don't have any of that here, for all we talk about is suffering, stress, the defilements, not-self. If we know with real mindfulness and discernment, we can scrape away our defilements, cravings, and attachments, and the good results will be right there inside us.

So now that we have this opportunity, we should make a concerted effort for the sake of our own progress. Don't let your life pass under the influence of defilement, craving, and attachment. Make an effort to correct yourself in this area every day, every moment, and you're sure to progress in your practice of destroying your defilements and disbanding your suffering and stress at all times. This business of sacrificing defilements or sacrificing your sense of self is very important because it gives rewards—peace, normalcy, freedom with every moment—*right here in the heart*. The practice is thus something really worthy of interest. If you're not interested in the practice of searching out and destroying the diseases of defilement, of your own suffering and stress, you'll have to stay stuck there in repeated suffering along with every other ignorant person in the world.

When Māra—the Tempter—tried to stop the Buddha's efforts by telling him that within seven days he would become a Universal Emperor, the Buddha answered, "I know already! Don't try to deceive me or tempt me." Because the Buddha had the ability to know such things instantly for himself, Māra was continually defeated. But what about you? Are you a disciple of the Lord Buddha or of Māra? Whenever temptation appears—there you go, following him hook, line, and sinker, with no sense of weariness or dispassion at all. If we're really disciples of the Buddha we have to go *against* the flow of defilement, craving, and attachment, establishing ourselves in good qualities—beginning with morality, which forms the ideal principle for protecting ourselves. Then we can gain release from suffering by working from the level of the precepts on to mental calm and then using discernment to see inconstancy, stress, and not-self. This is a high level of discernment, you know: the discernment that penetrates not-self.

At any rate, the important point is that you not believe your defilements. Even though you may still have the effluents of ignorance or craving in your mind, always keep making use of mindfulness and discernment as your means of knowing, letting go, scrubbing things clean. When these effluents come to tempt you, simply stop. Let go. Refuse to go along with them. If you believe them when they tell you to latch onto things, you'll simply continue being burned and agitated by desire. But if you don't go along with them, the desires in the mind will gradually loosen, subside, and eventually cease.

So in training the mind, you have to take desire as your battlefield in the same way you would in treating an addiction: If you aren't intent on defeating it, there's no way you can escape being a slave to it. We have to use mindfulness as a protective shield and discernment as our weapon to cut through and destroy our desires. In that way our practice will bring steady progress, enabling us to keep abreast of defilement, craving and attachment with more and more precision.

If, in your practice, you can read and decipher the mind, you'll find your escape route, following the footsteps of the Noble Ones. But as long as you don't see it, you'll think that there are no paths, no fruitions, no *nibbāna. Only when you can disband the defilements will you know.* You really have to be able to disband them in order to know for yourself that the paths, fruitions, and *nibbāna* really exist and really can disband suffering and stress. This is something you have to know for yourself. It's timeless: No matter what the time or season, whenever you have the mindfulness to stop and let go, there's no suffering. As you learn to do this over and over, more and more frequently, the defilements grow weaker and weaker. This is why it's *ehipassiko*—something you can invite other people to come and see, for all people who do this can disband defilement and suffering. If they contemplate until they see inconstancy, stress, and not-self, they'll no longer have any attachments, and their minds will become Dhamma, will become free.

There's no need to get all excited about anyone outside—spirit entities or whatever—because success in the practice lies right here in the heart. Look into it until you penetrate clearly all the way through yourself, sweep away all your attachments, and then you'll have this *"ehipassiko"* within you. "Come and see! Come and see!" But if there's still any defilement, then it's, "Come and see! Come and see the defilements burning me!" It can work both ways, so beware. If you disband the defilements, let go, and come to a stop, then it's, "Come and see how the defilements are gone, how the mind is empty right here and now!" This is something anyone can know, something you can know thoroughly for yourself with no great difficulty.

Turning to look into the mind isn't all that difficult. You don't have to travel far to do it. You can watch it at any time, in any posture. True things and false are all there within you, but if you don't study yourself within, you won't know them—for you spend all your time studying outside, the things of the world that worldly people study. If you want to study the Dhamma, you have to turn around and come inside, watching right at the body, at feelings, at the mind, at mental qualities, until you know the truth that the body isn't you or yours; it's inconstant, stressful, and not-self. Feelings are inconstant, stressful, and not-self. The mind is inconstant, stressful, and not-self as well. Then look at the Dhamma of mental qualities: They're inconstant and stressful. They arise, persist, and pass away. If you don't latch on and can become free from any sense of self right here at mental qualities, the mind becomes free.

If you understand correctly, the mind is really easy to deal with. If you don't, it's the exact opposite. Like pushing a light switch: If you hit the "on" button, the light is immediately bright. With the "off" button, it's immediately dark. The same holds true with the mind. If your knowledge is wrong, it's dark. If your knowledge is right, it's bright. Then look to see if there's anything worth clinging to. If you really look, you'll see that there isn't, for all the things you can cling to are suf-fering and stress—affairs of ignorance, speculation, day-dreaming, taking issue with things, self, people, useless chat-ter, endless news reports. But if you focus on probing into the mind, there's nothing—nothing but letting go to be empty and free. This is where the Dhamma arises easily—as easily as defilements arise on the other side, simply that you're now looking from a different angle and have the choice: Do you want the dark angle or the bright? Should you stop or keep running? Should you be empty or entangled? It's yours to decide within you.

The Dhamma is something marvelous and amazing. If you start out with right understanding, you can understand all the way through. If you get snagged at any point, you can examine and contemplate things to see where you're still attached. Keep cross-examining back and forth, and then all will become clear.

We're already good at following the knowledge of defile-ment and craving, so now we have to follow the knowledge of mindfulness and discernment instead. Keep cross-exam-ining the defilements. Don't submit to them easily. You have to resist their power and refuse to fall in with them. That's when you'll really come to know. When you really know, everything stops. Craving stops, your wanderings stop, likes, hatreds—this knowledge sweeps everything away. But if you don't know, you keep gathering things up until you're thor-oughly embroiled: arranging this, adjusting that, wanting this and that, letting your sense of self rear its ugly head.

Think of it like this: You're a huge playhouse showing a true-to-life drama whose hero, heroine, and villains—which are conventional suppositions—are entirely within you. If you strip away all conventional suppositions and designations, what you have left is nothing but Dhamma: freedom, empti-ness. And simply being free and empty of any sense of self is enough to bring the whole show to an end.

PART IV

A Good Dose of Dhamma

For Meditators When They Are Ill

September 3, 1965

I

Normally, illness is something we all have, but the type of illness where you can still do your work isn't recognized as illness. It's called the normal human state all over the world. Yet really, when the body is in its normal state, it's still ill in and of itself—simply that people in general are unaware of the fact that it's the deterioration of physical and mental phenomena, continually, from moment to moment.

The way people get carried away with their thoughts and preoccupations while they're still strong enough to do this and do that: That's really complacency. They're no match at all for people lying in bed ill. People lying in bed ill are lucky because they have the opportunity to do nothing but contemplate stress and pain. Their minds don't take up anything else, don't go anywhere else. They can contemplate pain at all times—and let go of pain at all times as well.

Don't you see the difference? The "emptiness" of the mind when you're involved in activities is "play" emptiness. Imitation emptiness. It's not the real thing. But to contemplate inconstancy, stress, and not-selfness as it appears right inside you while you're lying right here, is very beneficial for you.

Just don't think that *you're* what's hurting. Simply see the natural phenomena of physical and mental events as they pass away, pass away. They're not you. They're not really yours. You don't have any real control over them.

Look at them! Exactly where do you have any control over them? This is true for everyone in the world. You're not the only one to whom it's happening. So whatever the disease there is in your body, it isn't important. What's important is the disease in the mind. Normally we don't pay too much attention to the fact that we have diseases in our minds, i.e. the diseases of defilement, craving, and attachment. We pay attention only to our physical diseases, afraid of all the horrible things that can happen to the body. But no matter how much we try to stave things off with our fears, when the time comes for things to happen, no matter what medicines you have to treat the body, they can give you only temporary respite. Even the people in the past who *didn't* suffer from heavy diseases are no longer with us. They've all had to part from their bodies in the end.

So when you continually contemplate in this way, it makes you see the truth of inconstancy, stress, and not-selfness correctly within you. And you'll have to grow more and more disenchanted with things, step by step.

When you give it a try and let go, who's there? Are *you* the one hurting, or is it simply an affair of the Dhamma? You have to examine this very carefully to see that it's not really you that's hurting. *The disease isn't your disease. It's a disease of the body,* a disease of physical form. In the end, physical form and mental events have to change, to be stressful in the change, to be not-self in the change and the stress. But you must focus on them, watch them, and contemplate them so that they're clear. Make this knowledge really clear, and right there is where you'll gain release from all suffering and stress. Right there is where you'll put an end to all suffering and stress. As for the aggregates, they'll continue to arise, age, grow ill, and pass away in line with their own affairs. When their causes and conditions run out, they die and go into their coffin.

Some people, when they're healthy and complacent, die suddenly and unexpectedly without knowing what's happening to them. Their minds are completely oblivious to what's going on. This is much worse than the person lying ill in bed who has pain to contemplate as a means of developing disenchantment. So you don't have to be afraid of pain. If it's going to be there, let it be there—but don't let the mind be in pain with it. And then look—right now—is the mind empty of "me" and "mine"?

Keep looking on in. Keep looking on in so that things are really clear, and that's enough. You don't have to go knowing anything anywhere else. When you can cure the disease, or the pain lightens, that's something normal. When it doesn't lighten, that's normal, too. But if the heart is simply empty of "me" and "mine," there will be no pain within it. As for the pain in the aggregates, don't give it a second thought.

So see yourself as lucky. Lying here, dealing with the disease, you have the opportunity to practice insight meditation with every moment. It doesn't matter whether you're here in the hospital or at home. Don't let there be any real sense in the mind that you're in the hospital or at home. *Let the mind be in the emptiness,* empty of all labels and meanings. You don't have to label yourself as being anywhere at all.

This is because the aggregates are not where you are. They're empty of any indwelling person. They're empty of any "me" or "mine." When the mind is like this, it doesn't need anything at all. It doesn't have to be here or go there or anywhere at all. This is the absolute end of suffering and stress....

The mind, when it doesn't get engrossed with the taste of pleasure or pain, is free in and of itself, in line with its own nature. But I ask that you watch it carefully, the behavior of this mind as it's empty in line with its own nature, not concocting any desires for anything, not wanting pleasure or trying to push away pain.

When the mind is empty in line with its nature, there's no sense of ownership in it; there are no labels for itself. No matter what thoughts occur to it, it sees them as insubstantial, as empty of self. There's simply a sensation that then passes away. A sensation that then passes away, and that's all.

So you have to watch the phenomena that arise and pass away. In other words, you have to watch the phenomenon of the present continuously—and the mind will be empty, in that it gives no meanings or labels to the arising and passing away. As for the arising and passing away, that's a characteristic of the aggregates that has to appear as part of their normal nature—simply that the mind isn't involved, doesn't latch on. This is the point you can make use of.

You can't go preventing pleasure and pain, you can't keep the mind from labeling things and forming thoughts, *but you can put these things to a new use.* If the mind labels a pain, saying, "I hurt," you have to read the label carefully, contemplate it until you see that it's wrong. If the label were right, it would have to say that the pain isn't me, it's empty. Or if there's a thought that "I'm in pain," this type of thinking is also wrong. You have to take a new approach to your thinking, to see that thinking is inconstant, stressful, and not yours.

So whatever arises, investigate and let go of what's right in front of you. Just make sure that you don't cling, and the mind will keep on being empty in line with its nature. If no thoughts are bothering you, there may be strong pain, or the mind may be developing an abnormal mood, but whatever is happening, you have to look right in, look all the way in to the sensation of the mind. Once you have a sense of the empty mind, then if there's any disturbance, any sense of irritation, you'll know that the knowledge giving rise to it is wrong knowledge, in and of itself. Right knowledge will immediately take over, making the wrong knowledge disband.

In order to hold continuously to this foundation of knowing, you first have to start out by exercising restraint over the mind, at the same time that you focus your attention and contemplate the phenomenon of stress and pain. Keep this up until the mind can maintain its stance in the clear emptiness of the heart. If you can do this all the way to the end, the final disbanding of suffering will occur right there, right where the mind is empty.

But you have to keep working at this continuously. Whenever pain arises, regardless of whether it's strong or not, don't label it or give it any meaning. Even if pleasure arises, don't label it as *your* pleasure. Just keep letting it go, and the mind will gain release—empty of all clinging or attachment to "selfness" with each and every moment. You have to apply all your mindfulness and energy to this at all times.

You should see yourself as fortunate, that you're lying here ill, contemplating pain, for you have the opportunity to develop the Path in full measure, gaining insight and letting things go. Nobody has a better opportunity than you do right now. People running around, engaged in their affairs: Even if they say their minds are disengaged, they're really no match for you. A person lying ill in bed has the opportunity to develop insight with every in-and-out breath. It's a sign that you haven't wasted your birth as a human being, because you're practicing the teachings of the Lord Buddha to the point where you gain clear knowledge into the true nature of things in and of themselves.

The true nature of things, on the outside level, refers to the phenomenon of the present, the changing of the five aggregates. You can decipher their code, decipher their code until you get disenchanted with them, lose your taste for them, and let them go. When the mind is in this state, the next step is to contemplate it skillfully to see how it's empty, all the way to the ultimate emptiness—the kind of emptiness that goes clearly into the true nature lying most deeply inside where there is no concocting of thoughts, no arising, no passing away, no changing at all.

When you correctly see the nature of things on the outer level until it is all clear to you, the mind will let go, let go. That's when you automatically see clearly the nature of what lies on the inner level—empty of all cycling through birth and death, with nothing concocted at all....The emptiest extreme of emptiness, with no labels, no meanings, no clingings or attachments. All I ask is that you see this clearly within your own mind.

The ordinary emptiness of the mind is useful on one level, but that's not all there is. True emptiness is empty until it reaches the true nature of things on the inner level—something really worth ferreting out, really worth coming to know....

This is something you have to know for yourself.... There are really no words to describe it ... but we can talk about it by way of guidance, because it may happen that ultimately you let go of everything, in what's called disbanding without trace.

The mind's point of disbanding without trace, if you keep developing insight every day, every moment like this, will happen on its own. The mind will know on its own. So don't let the mind bother itself by getting preoccupied with pleasure or pain. Focus on penetrating into the mind in and of itself. Be relentless about it.

Do you see how different this is from when you're running around strong and healthy, thinking about this, that, and the other thing?... This is why there's no harm in having lots of pain. *The harm is in our stupidity* in giving labels and meanings to things. People in general tend to reflect on the fleeting nature of life with reference to other people, when someone else grows sick or dies, but they rarely reflect on the fleeting nature of their own lives. Or else they reflect for just a moment and then forget all about it, getting completely involved in their other preoccupations. They don't bring these truths inward, to reflect on the inconstancy occurring within themselves with every moment.

The fact that they can still do this and that, think this and that, say this and that, makes them lose all perspective. When you practice insight meditation, it's not something that you take a month or two off to do on a special retreat. That's not the real thing. It's no match for what you're doing right now, for here you can do it all day every day and all night, except when you sleep. Especially when the pain is strong, it's really good for your meditation, because it gives you the chance to know once and for all what inconstancy is like, what stress and suffering are like, what your inability to control things is like.

You have to find out right here, right in front of you, so don't try to avoid the pain. Practice insight so as to see the true nature of pain, its true nature as Dhamma, and then keep letting it go. If you do this, there's no way you can go wrong. This is the way to release from suffering.

And you ought to know by now that it's something you have to do before you die, not something you wait to do when you die or are just about to die. It's something you simply keep on doing, keep on "insighting." When the disease lessens, you "insight" it. When it grows heavy, you "insight" it. If you keep on developing insight like this, the mind will get over its stupidity and delusion. In other words, things like craving and defilement won't dare hassle the mind the way they used to....

So you have to give it your all—all your mindfulness, all your energy—now that you have the opportunity to practice the Dhamma. Let this be your last lifetime. Don't let there be anything born again. If you're born again, things will come back again just as they are now. The same old stuff, over and over and over again. Once there's birth, there has to be ageing, illness, and death, in line with your defilements, experiencing the good and bad results they keep churning out. It's a cycle of suffering. So the best thing is to gain release from birth. Don't let yourself want anything any more. Don't let yourself want anything any more, for all your wants fall in with what's inconstant, stressful, and not-self.

Wanting is simply a form of defilement and craving. You have to disband these things right at the instigator: the wanting that's nothing but craving for sensuality, craving for becoming, or craving for no becoming—the germs of birth in the heart. So focus in and contemplate at the right spot, seeing that even though craving may be giving rise to birth at sensory contact, you can set your knowing right at the mind, right at consciousness itself, and let there just be *the knowing that lets go of knowing.* This is something to work at until you have it mastered.

Setting your knowing at the mind, letting go of knowing like this, is something very beneficial. There's no getting stuck, no grabbing hold of your knowledge or views. If the knowledge is right, you let it go. If the knowledge is wrong, you let it go. This is called knowing letting go of knowing without going and getting entangled. This kind of knowing keeps the mind from latching onto whatever arises. As soon as you know something, you let it go. As soon as you know something, you've let it go. The mind just keeps on staying empty—empty of mental formations and thoughts, empty of every sort of illusion that could affect the mind. It quickly sees through them and lets them go, knows and lets go, without holding onto anything. All it has left is the emptiness....

You've already seen results from your practice, step by step, from contemplating things and letting them go, letting go even of the thought that *you* are the one in pain, that *you* are the one who's dying. The pain and the dying are an affair of the aggregates, pure and simple. When this knowledge is clear and sure—that it's not "my" affair, there's no "me" in there—there's just an empty mind: an empty mind, empty of any label for itself. This is the nature of the mind free of the germs that used to make it assume this and that. They're dead now. Those germs are now dead because we've contemplated them.

We've let go. We've set our knowing right at the mind and let go of whatever knowing has arisen, all along to the point where the mind is empty. Clear. In and of itself....

Consciousness, when you're aware of it inwardly, arises and passes away by its very own nature. There's no real essence to it—this is what you see when you look at the elemental property of consciousness *(viññāṇa-dhātu)*, pure and simple. When it's not involved with physical or mental phenomena, it's simply aware of itself—aware, pure and simple. That's called the mind pure and simple, or the property of consciousness pure and simple, in and of itself, and it lets go of itself. When you're told to know and to let go of the knowing, it means to know the consciousness that senses things and then lets go of itself.

As for the aggregate of consciousness *(viññāṇa-khandha)*, that's a trouble-making consciousness. The germs that keep piling things on lie in this kind of consciousness, which wants to hang onto a sense of self. Even though it can let go of physical pain, or of physical and mental events in general, it still hangs onto a sense of self. So when you're told to know the letting go of knowing, it means to let go of this kind of consciousness, to the point where consciousness has no label for itself. That's when it's empty. If you understand this, or can straighten out the heart and mind from this angle, there won't be anything left. Pain, suffering, stress—all your preoccupations—will become entirely meaningless. There will be no sense of good or bad or anything at all. Dualities will no longer be able to have an effect. If you know in this way—the knowing that lets go of knowing, consciousness pure and simple—it prevents any possible fashioning of the mind.

The dualities that fashion good and bad: There's really nothing to them. They arise, and that's all there is to them; they disband, and that's all there is to them. So now we come to know the affairs of the dualities that fashion the mind into spirals, that fashion the mind or consciousness into endless cycles. When you know the knowing that lets go of knowing, right at consciousness in and of itself, dualities have no more meaning. There's no more latching onto the labels of good and bad, pleasure and pain, true and false, or whatever. You just keep on letting go....

Even this knowing that lets go of knowing has no label for itself, saying, "I know," or "I see." But this is something that lies a little deep, that you have to make an effort to see clearly and rightly. You have to keep looking in a shrewd way. The shrewdness of your looking: That's something very important, for only that can lead to Awakening. Your knowledge has to be shrewd. Skillful. *Make sure that it's shrewd and skillful.* Otherwise your knowledge of the true nature of things—on the inner or outer levels—won't really be clear. It'll get stuck on just the elementary levels of emptiness, labeling and latching onto them in a way that just keeps piling things on. That kind of emptiness simply can't compare with this kind—the knowing that lets go of knowing right at consciousness pure and simple. Make sure that this kind of knowing keeps going continuously. If you slip for a moment, just get right back to it. You'll see that when you don't latch onto labels and meanings, thoughts of good and bad will just come to a stop. They'll disband. So when the Buddha tells us to see the world as empty, this is the way we see.

The emptiness lies in the fact that the mind doesn't give meaning to things, doesn't fashion things, doesn't cling. It's empty right at this kind of mind. Once you're correctly aware of this kind of empty mind, you'll no longer get carried away by anything at all. But if you don't really focus down like this, there will be only a little smattering of emptiness, and then you'll find yourself getting distracted by this and that, spoiling the emptiness. That kind of emptiness is emptiness in confusion. You're still caught up in confusion because you haven't contemplated down to the deeper levels. You simply play around with emptiness, that's all. The deeper levels of emptiness require that you focus in and keep on looking until you're thoroughly clear about the true nature of things in the phenomenon of the present arising and disbanding right in front of you. This kind of mind doesn't get involved, doesn't latch on to meanings or labels.

If you see this kind of emptiness correctly, there are no more issues, no more labels for anything in this heap of physical and mental phenomena. When the time comes for it all to fall apart, there's nothing to get excited about, nothing to get upset about, for that's the way it has to go by its nature. *Only if we latch onto it will we suffer....*

The Dhamma is right here in our body and mind, simply that we don't see it—or that we see it wrongly, latching on and making ourselves suffer. If we look at things with the eyesight of mindfulness and discernment, what is there to make us suffer? Why is there any need to fear pain and death? Even if we do fear them, what do we accomplish? Physical and mental phenomena have to go their own way—inconstant in their own way, stressful in their own way, beyond our control in their own way. So what business do we have in reaching out, latching on, and saying that their stress and pain is *our* stress and pain? If we understand that the latching on is what makes us suffer over and over, with each and every breath, then all we have to do is let go and we'll see how there is release from suffering right before our very eyes....

So keep on looking in to know, in the way I've described, right at the mind. But don't go labeling it as a "mind" or anything at all. Just let there be things as they are, in and of themselves, pure and simple. That's enough. You don't need to have any meanings or labels for anything at all. That will be the end of all suffering.... When things disband in the ultimate way, they disband right at the point of the elemental property of consciousness free of the germs that will give rise to anything further. That's where everything comes to an end, with no more rebirth or redeath of any kind at all....

The practice is something you have to do for yourself. If you know things clearly and correctly with your own mindfulness and discernment, that's your tool, well sharpened, in hand. If the mind is trained to be sharp, with mindfulness and discernment as its tool for contemplating itself, then defilement, craving, and attachment will keep getting weeded out and cleared away. You can look and see, from the amount you've already practiced: Aren't they already cleared away to some extent? The mind doesn't have to worry about anything, doesn't have to get involved with anything else. Let go of everything outside and then *keep* letting go until the mind lets go of itself. When you do this, how can you *not* see the great worth of the Dhamma?...

So I ask that this mind empty of attachment, empty of any sense of self whatsoever, be clear to you until you see that it's nothing but Dhamma. Get so that it's nothing but Dhamma, perfectly plain to your awareness. May this appear to you, as it is on its own, with each and every moment.

II

Listening to the Dhamma when the mind has already reached a basic level of emptiness is very beneficial. It's like an energizing tonic, for when we're sick there's bound to be pain disturbing us; but if we don't pay it any attention, it simply becomes an affair of the body, without involving the mind at all. Notice this as you're listening: The mind has let go of the pain to listen to the words, leaving the pain to its own affairs. The mind is then empty....

Once the mind honestly sees the truth that all compounded things are inconstant, it will have to let go of its attachments. The problem here is that we haven't yet really seen this, or haven't yet reflected on it in a skillful way. Once we do, though, the mind is always ready to grow radiant. Clear knowing makes the mind immediately radiant. So keep careful watch on things. Even if you don't know very much, just be aware of the mind as it maintains a balance in its basic level of neutrality and emptiness. Then it won't be able to fashion the pains in the body into any great issues, and you won't have to be attached to them.

So keep your awareness of the pain right at the level where it's no more than a mere sensation in the body. It can be the body's pain, but don't let the mind be in pain with it. If you *do* let the mind be in pain with it, that will pile things on, layer after layer. So the first step is to protect the mind, to let things go, then turn inward to look for the deepest, most innermost part of your awareness and stay right there. *You don't have to get involved with the pains outside.* If you simply try to endure them, they may be too much for you to endure. So look for the aspect of the mind that lies deep within, and you'll be able to put everything else aside.

Now, if the pains are the sort that you can watch, then make an effort to watch them. The mind will stay at its normal neutrality, calm with its own inner emptiness, watching the pain as it changes and passes away. But if the pain is too extreme, then turn around and go back inside; for if you can't handle it, then craving is going to work its way into the picture, wanting to push the pain away and to gain pleasure. This will keep piling on, piling on, putting the mind in a horrible turmoil.

So start out by solving the problem right at hand. If the pain is sudden and sharp, immediately turn around and focus all your attention on the mind. You don't want to have anything to do with the body, anything to do with the pains in the body. You don't look at them, you don't pay them any attention. Focus on staying with the innermost part of your awareness. Get to the point where you can see the pure state of mind that isn't in pain with the body, and keep it constantly clear.

Once this is constantly clear, then no matter how much pain there is in the body, it's simply an affair of mental and physical events. The mind, though, isn't involved. It puts all these things aside. It lets go.

When you're adept at this, it's a very useful skill to have, for the important things in life don't lie outside. They lie entirely within the mind. If we understand this properly, we won't have to go out to grab this or that. We won't have to latch onto anything at all—because if we do latch on, we simply cause ourselves needless suffering. The well-being of the mind lies at the point where it doesn't latch onto anything, where it doesn't want anything. That's where our well-being lies—the point where all suffering and stress disband right at the mind....

If we don't really understand things, though, the mind won't be willing to let things go. It will keep on holding tight, for it finds so much flavor in things outside. Whatever involves pain and stress: That's what it likes.

We have to focus on contemplating and looking, looking at the illusions in the mind, the wrong knowledge and opinions that cover it up and keep us from seeing the aspect of the mind that's empty and still by its own internal nature. Focus on contemplating the opinions that give rise to the complicated attachments that bury the mind until it's in awful straits. See how mental events—feelings, perceptions, and thought-formations—condition the mind, condition the property of consciousness until it's in terrible shape.

This is why it's so important to ferret out the type of knowing that lets go of knowing, i.e. that knows the property of consciousness pure and simple when mental events haven't yet come in to condition it, or when it hasn't gone out to condition mental events. Right here is where things get really interesting—in particular, the thought-formations that condition consciousness. They come from ignorance, right? It's because of our not knowing, or our wrong knowing, that they're able to condition things.

So I ask you to focus on this ignorance, this not-knowing. If you can know the characteristics of not-knowing, this same knowledge will know both the characteristics of thought-formations as they go about their conditioning and how to disband them. This requires adroit contemplation because it's something subtle and deep.

But no matter how subtle it may be, the fact that we've developed our mindfulness and discernment to this point means that we have to take an interest in it. If we don't, there's no way we can put an end to stress or gain release from it.

Or, if you want, you can approach it like this: Focus exclusively on the aspect of the mind that's constantly empty. If any preoccupations appear to it, be aware of the characteristics of bare sensation when forms make contact with the eye, or sounds with the ear, and so forth. There's a bare sensation, and then it disbands before it can have any such meaning as "good" or "bad." *If there's just the bare sensation that then disbands, there's no suffering.*

Be observant of the moment when forms make contact with the eye. With some things, if you're not interested in them, no feelings of liking or disliking arise. But if you get interested or feel that there's a meaning to the form, sound, smell, taste, or tactile sensation, you'll notice that as soon as you give a meaning to these things, attachment is already there.

If you stop to look in this way, you'll see that attachment is something subtle, because it's there even in the simple act of giving meaning. If you look superficially, you won't see that it's attachment—even though, on a subtle level, that's what it is. *As soon as there's a meaning, there's already attachment.* This requires that you have to be good and observant—because in the contact at the eyes and ears that we take so much for granted, many sleights-of-hand happen all at once, which means that we aren't aware of the characteristics of the consciousness that knows each individual sensation. We have to be very observant if we want to be able to know these things. If we aren't aware on this level, everything will be tied up in attachment. These things will keep sending their reports into the mind, conditioning and concocting all kinds of issues that leave the mind, or consciousness, in utter turmoil.

So if we want to look purely inside, we have to be very, very observant, because things inside are subtle, elusive, and sensitive. When the mind seems empty and neutral: That's when you really have to keep careful watch and control over it, so as to see clearly the sensation of receiving contact. There's contact, pure and simple, then it disbands, and the mind is empty. Neutral and empty. Once you know this, you'll know what the mind is like when it isn't conditioned by the power of defilement, craving, and attachment. We can use this emptiness of the mind as our standard of comparison, and it will do us a world of good....

Ultimately, you'll see the emptiness of all sensory contacts, as in the Buddha's teaching that we should see the world as empty. What he meant is for us to observe bare sensations simply arising and passing away, knowing what consciousness is like when it does nothing more than simply receive contact. If you can see this, the next step in the practice won't be difficult at all—because you've established neutrality right from the start. The act of receiving contact is no longer complicated: The mind no longer grabs hold of things, no longer feels any likes or dislikes. It's simply quiet and aware all around within itself at all times. Even if you can do this much, you find that you benefit from not letting things get complex, from not letting issues get concocted through the power of defilement, craving, and attachment. Even just this much gets rid of lots of problems.

Then when you focus further in to see the nature of all phenomena that are known through sensory contact, you'll see that there's simply bare sensation with nothing at all worth getting attached to. If you look with the eyes of true mindfulness and discernment, you'll have to see emptiness—even though the world is full of things. The eye sees lots of forms, the ear hears lots of sounds, but the mind no longer gives them meanings. At the same time, things have no meanings in and of themselves.

The only important thing is the mind. *All issues come from the mind that goes out and gives things meanings* and gives rise to attachment, creating stress and suffering for itself. So you have to look until you see all the way through. Look outward until you see all the way out, and inward until you see all the way in, all the way until you penetrate inconstancy, stress, and not-selfness. See things as they are, in and of themselves, in line with their own nature, without any meanings or attachments. Then there won't be any issues. The mind will be empty—clean and bright—without your having to do anything to it.

Now, the fact that the mind has the viruses of ignorance, or of the craving that can easily give rise to issues, means that we can't be careless. In the beginning, you have to supervise things carefully so that you can see the craving that arises at the moment of contact—say, when there's a feeling of pain. If you don't label it as meaning *your* pain, craving won't get too much into the act. But if you do give it that meaning, then there will be the desire to push the pain away or to have pleasure come in its place.

All this, even though we've never gotten anything true and dependable from desiring. The pleasure we get from our desires doesn't last. It fools us and then changes into something else. Pain fools us and then changes into something else. But these changes keep piling up and getting very complicated in the mind, and this is what keeps the mind ignorant: It's been conditioned in so many ways that it gets confused, deluded, dark, and smoldering.

All kinds of things are smoldering in here.... This is why the principle of the knowing that lets go of knowing is such an important tool. Whatever comes at you, the knowing that lets go of knowing is enough to get you through. It takes care of everything. If you let it slip, simply get back to the same sort of knowing. See for yourself how far it will take you, how much it can keep the mind neutral and empty.

You can come to see this bit by bit. In the moments when the mind isn't involved with very much, when it's at a basic level of normalcy—empty, quiet, whatever—keep careful watch over it and analyze it as well. Don't let it linger in an oblivious state of indifference, or else it will lose its balance. If you're in an oblivious state, then as soon as there's contact at any of the sense doors, there's sure to be attachment or craving giving rise to things the instant in which feeling appears. You have to focus on keeping watch of the changes, the behavior of the mind at every moment. As soon as your mindfulness lapses, get back immediately to your original knowing. We're all bound to have lapses—all of us—because the effluent of ignorance, the most fundamental of the effluents, is still there in the mind.

This is why we have to keep working at our watchfulness, our investigation, our focused awareness, so that they keep getting clearer and clearer. Make your mind ripe in mindfulness and discernment, continuously....

Once they're ripe enough for you to know things in a skillful way, you'll be able to disband the defilements the very moment they appear. As soon as you begin feeling likes and dislikes, you can deal with them before they amount to anything. This makes things a lot easier. If you allow them to condition the mind—making it irritated, murky, and stirred up to the point where it shows in your words and actions—then you're in terrible straits, falling into hell in this very lifetime.

The practice of the Dhamma requires that we be ingenious and circumspect right at the mind. The defilements are always ready to flatter us, to work their way into our favor. If we aren't skillful in our awareness, if we don't know how to keep the mind under careful supervision, we'll be no match for them—for there are so many of them. But if we do a thorough job of supervising the mind, the defilements will be afraid of us—afraid of our mindfulness and discernment, afraid of our awareness. Notice when the mind is empty, aware all around, with no attachments to anything at all: The defilements will hide out quiet, as if they weren't there at all.

But as soon as mindfulness slips, even just a little, they spring right up. They spring right up. If you recognize them for what they are the moment they spring up, they'll disband right there. This is a very useful skill to have. But if we let them turn into issues, they'll be hard to disband. That's when you have to bear with the fight and not give up.

Whatever happens, start out by bearing with it—*not simply to endure it, but so as to examine it,* to see what it's like, how it changes, how it passes away. We bear with things so that we can see through their deceits: the way they arise, persist, and disband on their own. If they disband while we're examining them and clearly seeing their deceitfulness, we can do away with them for good. This will leave the mind in a state of freedom and independence, empty entirely within itself.

If you can learn to see through things the moment they arise—what you might call your own little instantaneous awakenings—your awareness will keep getting brighter and brighter, stronger and more expansive all the time.

So work at them—these little instantaneous understandings—and eventually, when things come together in an appropriate way, you'll reach the point where, in an instant, defilements and effluents are abandoned, once and for all. When that happens, then—*nibbāna.* No more taking birth. But if you haven't yet reached that point, just keep sharpening your knives: your mindfulness and discernment. If they're dull, they won't be able to cut anything through, but whatever shape they're in, keep cutting through bit by bit whatever you can....

I ask that you keep at this: examining and understanding all around within the mind until you reach the point where everything is totally clear and you can let go of everything with the realization that nothing in the five aggregates or in physical and mental phenomena is *me* or *mine*. Keep trying to let go, and that will be enough. Each moment as they're taking care of you here in the hospital, do what has to be done for your illness, but make sure that there's this separate, special awareness exclusive to the mind—this knowing that simply lets go of itself. That will end all your problems right there....

PART V

Reading the Mind

DISCERNMENT vs. SELF-DECEPTION

It's important that we discuss the steps of the practice in training the mind, for the mind has all sorts of deceptions by which it fools itself. If you aren't skillful in investigating and seeing through them, they are very difficult to overcome even if you're continually mindful to keep watch over the mind. You have to make an effort to focus on contemplating these things at all times. Mindfulness on its own won't be able to give rise to any real knowledge. At best, it can give you only a little protection against the effects of sensory contact. If you don't make a focused contemplation, the mind won't be able to give rise to any knowledge within itself at all.

This is why you have to train yourself to be constantly aware all around. When you come to know anything for what it really is, there's nothing but letting go, letting go. On the beginning level, this means the mind won't give rise to any unwise or unprofitable thoughts. It will simply stop to watch, stop to know within itself at all times. If there's anything you have to think about, keep your thoughts on the themes of inconstancy, stress, and not-self. You have to keep the mind thinking and labeling solely in reference to these sorts of themes, for if your thinking and labeling are right, you'll come to see things rightly. If you go the opposite way, you'll have to think wrongly and label things wrongly, and that means you'll have to see things wrongly as well. This is what keeps the mind completely hidden from itself.

Now, when thoughts or labels arise in the mind, then if you focus on watching them closely you'll see that they're sensations—sensations of arising and disbanding, changeable, unreliable, and illusory. If you don't make an effort to keep a focused watch on them, you'll fall for the deceptions of thought-formation. In other words, the mind gives rise to memories of the past and fashions issues dealing with the past, but if you're aware of what's going on in time, you'll see that they're all illusory. There's no real truth to them at all. Even the meanings the mind gives to good and bad sensory contacts at the moment they occur: If you carefully observe and contemplate, you'll see that they're all deceptive. There's no real truth to them. But ignorance and delusion latch onto them all, and this drives the mind around in circles. In other words, it doesn't know what's what—how these things arise, persist, and disband—so it latches onto them and gets itself deceived on many, many levels. If you don't stop to focus and watch, there's no way you can see through these things at all.

But if the mind keeps its balance or stops to watch and know within itself, it can come to realize these things for what they are. When it realizes them, it can let them go automatically without being attached to anything. This is the knowledge that comes with true mindfulness and discernment: It knows and lets go. It doesn't cling. No matter what appears—good or bad, pleasure or pain—when the mind knows, it doesn't cling. *When it doesn't cling, there's no stress or suffering.* You have to keep hammering away at this point: When it doesn't cling, the mind can stay at normalcy. Empty. Undisturbed. Quiet and still. But if it doesn't read itself in this way, doesn't know itself in this way, it will fall for the deceits of defilement and craving. It will fashion up all sorts of complex and complicated things that it itself will have a hard time seeing through, for they'll have their ways of playing up to the mind to keep it attached to them, all of which is simply a matter of the mind's falling for the deceits of the defilements and cravings within itself. The fact that it isn't acquainted with itself—doesn't know how mental states arise and disband and take on objects—means that it loses itself in its many, many attachments.

There's nothing as hard to keep watch of as the mind, because it's so accustomed to wrong views and wrong opinions. This is what keeps it hidden from itself. But thanks to the teachings of the Buddha, we can gain knowledge into the mind, or into consciousness with its many layers and intricacies that, when you look into it deeply, you'll find to be empty—empty of any meaning in and of itself.

This is an emptiness that can appear clearly within consciousness. Even though it's hidden and profound, we can see into it by looking inward in a way that's quiet and still. The mind stops to watch, to know within itself. As for sensory contacts—sights, sounds, smells, tastes, and tactile sensations—it isn't interested, because it's intent on looking into consciousness pure and simple, to see what arises in there and how it generates issues. Sensations, thoughts, labels for pleasure and pain and so forth, are all natural phenomena that change as soon as they're sensed—and they're very refined. If you view them as being about this or that matter, you won't be able to know them for what they are. The more intricate the meanings you give them, the more lost you become—lost in the whorls of the cycle of rebirth.

The cycle of rebirth and the processes of thought-formation are one and the same thing. As a result, we whirl around and around, lost in many, many levels of thought-formation, not just one. The knowledge that would read the heart can't break through to know, for it whirls around and around in these very same thought-formations, giving them meanings in terms of this or that, and then latching onto them. If it labels them as good, it latches onto them as good. If it labels them as bad, it latches onto them as bad. This is why the mind stays entirely in the whorls of the cycle of rebirth, the cycle of thought-formation.

For this reason, to see these things clearly requires the effort to stop and watch, to stop and know *in an appropriate way*, in a way that's just right. At the same time, you have to use your powers of observation. *That's* what will enable you to read your own consciousness in a special way. Otherwise, if you latch onto the issues of thoughts and labels, they'll keep you spinning around. So you have to stop and watch, stop and know clearly by focusing down—*focusing down on the consciousness in charge*. In that way your knowledge will become skillful.

Ultimately, you'll see that there's nothing at all—just the arising and disbanding occurring every moment in emptiness. If there's no attachment, there are no issues. There's simply the natural phenomenon of arising and disbanding. But because we don't see things simply as natural phenomena, we see them as being true and latch onto them as our self, good, bad, and all sorts of other complicated things. This keeps us spinning around without knowing how to find a way out, what to let go of—we don't know. When we don't know, we're like a person who wanders into a jungle and doesn't know the way out, doesn't know what to do....

Actually what we have to let go of lies right smack in front of us: where the mind fashions things and gives them meanings so that it doesn't know the characteristics of arising and disbanding, pure and simple. If you can simply keep watching and knowing, without any need for meanings, thoughts, imaginings—simply watching the process of these things in and of itself—there won't be any issues. There's just the phenomenon of the present: arising, persisting, disbanding, arising, persisting, disbanding.... There's no special trick to this, but you have to stop and watch, stop and know within yourself *every moment*. Don't let your awareness stream away from awareness to outside preoccupations. Gather it in so it can know itself clearly—that there's nothing in there worth latching onto. It's all a bunch of deceits.

To know just this much is very useful for seeing the truth inside yourself. You'll see that consciousness is empty of any self. When you look at physical phenomena, you'll see them as elements, as empty of any self. You'll see mental phenomena as empty of any self, as elements of consciousness—and that if there's no attachment, no latching on, there's no suffering or stress....

So even if there's thinking going on in the mind, simply watch it, simply let it go, and its cycling will slow down. Fewer and fewer thought-formations will occur. Even if the mind doesn't stop completely, it will form fewer and fewer thoughts. You'll be able to stop to watch, stop to know more and more. And this way, you'll come to see the tricks and deceits of thought-formation, mental labels, pleasure and pain, and so on. You'll be able to know that there's really nothing inside—that the reason you were deluded into latching onto things was because of ignorance, and that you made yourself suffer right there in that very ignorance....

So you have to focus down on one point, one thing. Focusing on many things won't do. Keep mindfulness in place: stopping, knowing, seeing. Don't let it run out after thoughts and labels. But knowing in this way requires that you make the effort to stay focused—focused on seeing clearly, not just on making the mind still. Focus on seeing clearly. Look on in for the sake of seeing clearly ... and contemplate how to let go. The mind will become empty in line with its nature in a way that you'll know exclusively within.

A DIFFERENCE IN THE KNOWING

What can we do to see the aggregates—this mass of suffering and stress—clearly in a way that will enable us to cut attachment for them out of the mind? Why is it that people studying to be doctors can know everything in the body—intestines, liver, kidneys, and all—down to the details, and yet don't develop any dispassion or disenchantment for it—why? Why is it that undertakers can spend their time with countless corpses and yet not gain any insight at all? This shows that true insight is hard to attain. If there's no mindfulness and discernment to see things clearly for what they are, knowledge is simply a passing fancy. It doesn't sink in. The mind keeps latching onto its attachments.

But if the mind gains true insight to the point where it can relinquish its attachments, it can gain the paths and fruitions leading to *nibbāna*. This shows that there's a difference in the knowing. It's not that we have to know all the details like modern-day surgeons. All we have to know is that the body is composed of the four physical elements plus the elements of space and consciousness. If we *really* know just this much, we've reached the paths and their fruitions, while those who know all the details to the point where they can perform surgery don't reach any transcendent attainments at all....

So let's analyze the body into its elements so as to know them thoroughly. If we do, then when there are changes in the body and mind there won't be too much clinging. If we don't, our attachments will be fixed and strong and will lead to further states of being and birth in the future.

Now that we have the opportunity, we should contemplate the body and take it apart for a good look so as to get down to the details. Take the five basic meditation objects—hair of the head, hair of the body, nails, teeth, skin—and look at them carefully, one at a time. You don't have to take on all five, you know. Focus on the hair of the head to see that it belongs to the earth element, to see that its roots are soaked in blood and lymph under the skin. It's unattractive in terms of its color, its smell, and where it dwells. If you analyze and contemplate these things, you won't be deluded into regarding them as *your* hair, your nails, your teeth, your skin.

All of these parts are composed of the earth element mixed with water, wind, and fire. If they were purely earth they wouldn't last, because every part of the body has to be composed of all four elements for it to be a body. And then there's a mental phenomenon, the mind, in charge. These are things that follow in line with nature in every way—the arising, changing, and disbanding of physical and mental phenomena—but we latch onto them, seeing the body as ours, the mental phenomena as us: It's all us and ours. If we don't contemplate to see these things for what they are, we'll do nothing but cling to them.

This is what meditation is: seeing things clearly for what they are. It's not a matter of switching from topic to topic, for that would simply ensure that you wouldn't know a thing. But our inner character, under the sway of ignorance and delusion, doesn't like examining itself repeatedly. It keeps finding other issues to get in the way, so that we think constantly about other things. This is why we stay so ignorant and foolish.

Then why is it that we can know other things? Because they fall in line with what craving wants. To see things clearly for what they are would be to abandon craving, so it finds ways of keeping things hidden. It keeps changing, bringing in new things all the time, keeping us fooled all the time, so that we study and think about nothing but matters that add to the mind's suffering and stress. That's all that craving wants. As for the kind of study that would end the stress and suffering in the mind, it's always getting in the way.

This is why the mind is always wanting to shift to new things to know, new things to fall for. And this is why it's always becoming attached. So when it doesn't really know itself, you have to make a real effort to see the truth that the things within it aren't you or yours. Don't let the mind stop short of this knowledge: Make this a law within yourself. If the mind doesn't know the truths of inconstancy, stress, and not-self within itself, it won't gain release from suffering. Its knowledge will simply be worldly knowledge; it will follow a worldly path. It won't reach the paths and fruition leading to *nibbāna*.

So this is where the worldly and the transcendent part ways. If you comprehend inconstancy, stress, and not-self to the ultimate degree, that's the transcendent. If you don't get down to their details, you're still on the worldly level....

The Buddha has many teachings, but this is what they all come down to. The important principles of the practice—the four foundations of mindfulness, the Four Noble Truths—all come down to these characteristics of inconstancy, stress, and not-selfness. If you try to learn too many principles, you'll end up not getting any clear knowledge of the truth as it is. *If you focus on knowing just a little, you'll end up with more true insight than if you try knowing a lot of things.* It's through wanting to know a lot of things that we end up deluded. We wander around in our deluded knowledge, thinking and labeling things, *but knowledge that's focused and specific, when it really knows, is absolute.* It keeps hammering away at one point. There's no need to know a lot of things, for when you really know one thing, everything converges right there....

THE BALANCED WAY

In practicing the Dhamma, if you don't foster a balance between concentration and discernment, your thinking will end up going wild. If there's too much work at discernment, your thinking will go wild. If there's too much concentration, it just stays still and undisturbed without coming to any knowledge either. So you have to keep them in balance. Stillness has to be paired with discernment. Don't let there be too much of one or the other. Try to get them just right. That's when you'll be able to see things clearly all the way through. Otherwise, you'll stay as deluded as ever. You may want to gain discernment into too many things—and as a result, your thinking goes wild. The mind goes out of control. Some people keep wondering why discernment never arises in their practice, but when it does arise they really go off on a tangent. Their thinking goes wild, all out of bounds.

So when you practice, you have to observe in your meditation how you can make the mind still. Once it does grow still, it tends to get stuck there. Or it may grow empty, without any knowledge of anything: quiet, disengaged, at ease for a while, but without any discernment to accompany it. But if you *can* get discernment to accompany your concentration, that's when you'll really benefit. You'll see things all the way through and be able to let them go. If you're too heavy on the side of either discernment or stillness, you can't let go. The mind may come to know this or that, but it latches onto its knowledge. Then it knows still other things and latches onto them, too. Or else it simply stays perfectly quiet and latches onto *that*.

It's not easy to keep your practice on the middle way. If you don't use your powers of observation, it's especially hard. The mind will keep falling for things, sometimes right, sometimes wrong, because it doesn't observe what's going on. This isn't the path to letting go. It's a path that's stuck, caught up on things. If you don't know what it's stuck and caught up on, you'll remain foolish and deluded. So you have to make an effort at focused contemplation until you see clearly into inconstancy, stress, and not-self. This without a doubt is what will stop every moment of suffering and stress....

THE USES OF EQUANIMITY

The sensations of the mind are subtle and very volatile. Sometimes passion or irritation can arise completely independent of sensory contact, simply in line with the force of our character. For instance, there are times when the mind is perfectly normal, and all of a sudden there's irritation—or the desire to form thoughts and get engrossed in feelings of pain, pleasure, or equanimity. We have to contemplate these three kinds of feeling to see that they're inconstant and always changing, and to see that they are all stressful, so that the mind won't go and get engrossed in them. This business of getting engrossed is very subtle and hard to detect. It keeps us from knowing what's what because it's delusion pure and simple. Being engrossed in feelings of pleasure is something relatively easy to detect, but being engrossed in feelings of equanimity is hard to notice, because the mind is at equanimity in an oblivious way. This oblivious equanimity keeps us from seeing anything clearly.

So you have to focus on seeing feelings simply as feelings and pull the mind out of its state of being engrossed with equanimity. When there's a feeling of equanimity as the mind gathers and settles down, when it's not scattered around, use that feeling of equanimity in concentration as the basis for probing in to see inconstancy, stress, and not-self—for this equanimity in concentration at the fourth level of absorption (*jhana*) is the basis for liberating insight. Simply make sure that you don't get attached to the absorption.

If you get the mind to grow still in equanimity without focusing on gaining insight, it's simply a temporary state of concentration. So you have to focus on gaining clear insight either into inconstancy, into stress, or into not-selfness. That's when you'll be able to uproot your attachments. If the mind gets into a state of oblivious equanimity, it's still carrying fuel inside it. Then as soon as there's sensory contact, it flares up into attachment. So we have to follow the principles the Buddha laid down: Focus the mind into a state of absorption and then focus on gaining clear insight into the three characteristics. The proper way to practice is not to let yourself get stuck on this level or that—*and no matter what insights you may gain, don't go thinking that you've gained Awakening.* Keep looking. Keep focusing in to see if there are any further changes in the mind and, when there are, see the stress in those changes, the not-selfness of those changes. If you can know in this way, the mind will rise above feeling, no longer entangled in this level or that level—all of which are simply matters of speculation.

The important thing is that you try to see clearly. Even when the mind is concocting all sorts of objects in a real turmoil, focus on seeing all of its objects as illusory. Then stay still to watch their disbanding. Get so that it's clear to you that there's really nothing to them. They all disband. All that remains is the empty mind—the mind maintaining its balance in normalcy—and then focus in on examining *that.*

There are many levels to this process of examining the diseases in the mind, not just one. Even though you may come up with genuine insights every now and then, don't just stop there—and don't get excited about the fact that you've come to see things you never saw before. Just keep contemplating the theme of inconstancy in everything, without latching on, and then you'll come to even more penetrating insights....

So focus on in until the mind stops, until it reaches the stage of absorption called purity of mindfulness and equanimity. See what pure mindfulness is like. As for the feeling of equanimity, that's an affair of concentration. It's what the mindfulness depends on so that it too can reach equanimity. This is the stage where we gather the strength of our awareness in order to come in and know the mind. Get the mind centered, at equanimity, and then probe in to contemplate. That's when you'll be able to see....

A GLOB OF TAR

An important but subtle point is that even though we practice, we continue to fall for pleasant feelings, because feelings are illusory on many levels. We don't realize that they're changeable and unreliable. Instead of offering pleasure, they offer us nothing but stress—yet we're still addicted to them.

This business of feeling is thus a very subtle matter. Please try to contemplate it carefully—this business of latching onto feelings of pleasure, pain, or equanimity. You have to contemplate so as to see it clearly. And you have to experiment more than you may want to with pain. When there are feelings of physical pain or mental distress, the mind will struggle because it doesn't like pain. But when pain turns to pleasure, the mind likes it and is content with it, so it keeps on playing with feeling, even though, as we've already said, feeling is inconstant, stressful, and not really ours. But the mind doesn't see this. All it sees are feelings of pleasure, and it wants them.

Try looking into how feeling gives rise to craving. It's because we want pleasant feeling that craving whispers—whispers right there at the feeling. If you observe carefully, you'll see that this is very important, for this is where the paths and fruitions leading to *nibbāna* are attained, right here at feeling and craving. If we can extinguish the craving in feeling, that's *nibbāna*....

In the *Soḷasa Pañhā*, the Buddha said that defilement is like a wide and deep flood, but he then went on to summarize the practice to cross it simply as abandoning craving in every action. Now, right here at feeling is where we can practice to abandon craving, for the way we relish the flavor of feeling has many ramifications. This is where many of us get deceived, because we don't see feeling as inconstant. We want it to be constant. We want pleasant feelings to be constant. As for pain, we don't want it to be constant, but no matter how much we try to push it away, we still latch onto it.

This is why we have to focus on feeling, so that we can abandon craving right there in the feeling. If you don't focus here, the other paths you may follow will simply proliferate. So bring the practice close to home. When the mind changes, or when it gains a sense of stillness or calm that would rank as a feeling of pleasure or equanimity, try to see in what ways the pleasure or equanimity is inconstant, that it's not you or yours. When you can do this, you'll stop relishing that particular feeling. You can stop right there, right where the mind relishes the flavor of feeling and gives rise to craving. This is why the mind has to be fully aware of itself—all around, at all times—in its focused contemplation to see feeling as empty of self....

This business of liking and disliking feelings is a disease hard to detect, because our intoxication with feelings is so very strong. Even with the sensations of peace and emptiness in the mind, we're still infatuated with feeling. Feelings on the crude level—the violent and stressful ones that come with defilement—are easy to detect. But when the mind grows still—steady, cool, bright, and so on—we're still addicted to feeling. We want these feelings of pleasure or equanimity. We enjoy them. Even on the level of firm concentration or meditative absorption, there's attachment to the feeling....

This is the subtle magnetic pull of craving, which paints and plasters things over. This painting and plastering is hard to detect, because craving is always whispering inside us, "I want nothing but pleasant feelings." This is very important, for this virus of craving is what makes us continue to be re-born....

So explore to see how craving paints and plasters things, how it causes desires to form—the desires to get this or take that—and what sort of flavor it has that makes you so addicted to it, that makes it hard for you to pull away. You have to contemplate to see how craving fastens the mind so firmly to feelings that you never weary of sensuality or of pleasant feelings, no matter what the level. If you don't contemplate so as to see clearly that the mind is stuck right here at feeling and craving, it will keep you from gaining release....

We're stuck on feeling like a monkey stuck in a tar trap. They take a glob of tar and put it where a monkey will get its hand stuck in it and, in trying to pull free, the monkey gets its other hand, both feet, and finally its mouth stuck, too. Consider this: Whatever we do, we end up stuck right here at feeling and craving. We can't separate them out. We can't wash them off. If we don't grow weary of craving, we're like the monkey stuck in the glob of tar, getting ourselves more and more trapped all the time. So if we're intent on freeing ourselves in the footsteps of the arahants, we have to focus specifically on feeling until we can succeed at freeing ourselves from it. Even with painful feelings, we have to practice—for if we're afraid of pain and always try to change it to pleasure, we'll end up even more ignorant than before.

This is why we have to be brave in experimenting with pain—both physical pain and mental distress. When it arises in full measure, like a house afire, can we let go of it? We have to know both sides of feeling. When it's hot and burning, how can we deal with it? When it's cool and refreshing, how can we see through it? We have to make an effort to focus on both sides, contemplating until we know how to let go. Otherwise, we won't know anything, for all we want is the cool side, the cooler the better ... and when this is the case, how can we expect to gain release from the cycle of rebirth?

Nibbāna is the extinguishing of craving, and yet we like to stay with craving—so how can we expect to get anywhere at all? We'll stay right here in the world, right here with stress and suffering, for craving is a sticky sap. If there's no craving, there's nothing: no stress, no rebirth. But we have to watch out for it. It's a sticky sap, a glob of tar, a dye that's hard to wash out.

So don't let yourself get carried away with feeling. The crucial part of the practice lies here....

WHEN CONVENTIONAL TRUTHS COLLAPSE

In making yourself quiet, you have to be quiet on all fronts— quiet in your deeds, quiet in your words, quiet in your mind. Only then will you be able to contemplate what's going on inside yourself. If you aren't quiet, you'll become involved in external affairs and end up having too much to do and too much to say. This will keep your awareness or mindfulness from holding steady and firm. You have to stop doing, saying, or thinking anything that isn't necessary. That way your mindfulness will be able to develop continuously. Don't let yourself get involved in too many outside things.

In training your mindfulness to be continuous so that it will enable you to contemplate yourself, you have to be observant: When there's sensory contact, can the mind stay continuously undisturbed and at normalcy? Or does it still run out into liking and disliking? Being observant in this way will enable you to read yourself, to know yourself. If mindfulness is firmly established, the mind won't waver. If it's not yet firm, the mind will waver in the form of liking and disliking. You have to be wary of even the slightest wavering. Don't let yourself think that the slight waverings are unimportant, or else they'll become habitual.

Being uncomplacent means that you have to watch out for the details, the little things, the tiny flaws that arise in the mind. If you can do this, you'll be able to keep your mind protected—better than giving all your attention to the worthless affairs of the outside world. So really try to be careful. Don't get entangled in sensory contact. This is something you have to work at mastering. If you focus yourself exclusively in the area of the mind like this, you'll be able to contemplate feelings in all their details. You'll be able to see them clearly, to let them go.

So focus your practice right at feelings of pleasure, pain, and neither-pleasure-nor-pain. Contemplate how to leave them alone, simply as feelings, without relishing them—*for if you relish feelings, that's craving.* Desires for this and that will seep in and influence the mind so that it gets carried away with inner and outer feelings. This is why you have to be quiet—quiet in a way that doesn't let the mind become attached to the flavors of feelings, quiet in a way that uproots their influence.

The desire for pleasure is like a virus deep in our character. What we're doing here is to make the mind stop taking pleasant feelings into itself and stop pushing painful feelings away. Our addiction to taking in pleasant feelings is what makes us dislike painful feelings and push them away, so don't let the mind love pleasure and resist pain. Let it be undisturbed by both. Give it a try. If the mind can let go of feelings so that it's above pleasure, pain, and neither-pleasure-nor-pain, that means it's not stuck on feeling. And then try to observe: How can it *stay* unaffected by feelings? This is something you have to work at mastering in order to release your grasp on feelings once and for all, so that you won't latch onto physical pain or mental distress as being you or yours.

If you don't release your grasp on feeling, you'll stay attached to it, both in its physical and in its mental forms. If there's the pleasure of physical ease, you'll be attracted to it. As for the purely mental feeling of pleasure, that's something you'll really want, you'll really love. And then you'll be attracted to the mental perceptions and labels that accompany the pleasure, the thought-formations and even the consciousness that accompany the pleasure. You'll latch onto all of these things as you or yours.

So analyze physical and mental pleasure. Take them apart to contemplate how to let them go. Don't fool yourself into relishing them. As for pain, don't push it away. *Let pain simply be pain, let pleasure simply be pleasure.* Let them simply fall into the category of feelings. Don't go thinking that *you* feel pleasure, that *you* feel pain. If you can let go of feeling in this way, you'll be able to gain release from suffering and stress *because you'll be above and beyond feeling.* This way, when ageing, illness, and death come, you won't latch onto them thinking that *you* are ageing, that *you* are ill, that *you* are dying. You'll be able to release these things from your grasp.

If you can contemplate purely in these terms—that the five aggregates are inconstant, stressful, and not-self—you won't enter into them and latch onto them as "me" or "mine." If you don't analyze them in this way, you'll be trapped in dying. Even your bones, skin, flesh, and so forth will become "mine." This is why we're taught to contemplate death—so that we can make ourselves aware that death doesn't mean that *we* die. You have to contemplate until you really know this. Otherwise, you'll stay trapped right there. You must make yourself sensitive in a way that sees clearly how your bones, flesh, and skin are empty of any self. That way you won't latch onto them. The fact that you still latch onto them shows that you haven't really seen into their inconstancy, stress, and not-selfness.

When you see the bones of animals, they don't have much meaning, but when you see the bones of people, your perception labels them: "That's a person's skeleton. That's a person's skull." If there are a lot of them, they can really scare you. When you see the picture of a skeleton or of anything that shows the inconstancy and not-selfness of the body, and you don't see clear through it, you'll get stuck at the level of skeleton and bones. Actually, there are no bones at all. They're empty, nothing but elements. You have to penetrate into the bones so that they're elements. Otherwise, you'll get stuck at the level of skeleton. And since you haven't seen through it, it can make you distressed and upset. This shows that you haven't penetrated into the Dhamma. You're stuck at the outer shell because you haven't analyzed things into their elements.

When days and nights pass by, they're not the only things that pass by. The body constantly decays and falls apart, too. The body decays bit by bit, but we don't realize it. Only after it's decayed a lot—when the hair has gone grey and the teeth fall out—do we realize that it's old. This is knowledge on a crude and really blatant level. But as for the gradual decaying that goes on quietly inside, we aren't aware of it.

As a result, we cling to the body as being us—every single part of it. Its eyes are *our* eyes, the sights they see are the things *we* see, the sensation of seeing is something *we* sense. We don't see these things as elements. Actually, the element of vision and the element of form make contact. The awareness of the contact is the element of consciousness: the mental phenomenon that senses sights, sounds, smells, tastes, tactile sensations, and all. This we don't realize, which is why we latch onto everything—eyes, ears, nose, tongue, body, intellect —as being us or ours. Then, when the body decays, we feel that *we* are growing old; when it dies and mental phenomena stop, we feel that *we* die.

Once you've taken the elements apart, though, there's nothing. These things lose their meaning on their own. *They're simply physical and mental elements, without any illness or death.* If you don't penetrate into things this way, you stay deluded and blind. For instance, when we chant *"jarā-dhammāmhi*—I am subject to death"—that's simply to make us mindful and uncomplacent in the beginning stages of the practice. When you reach the stage of insight meditation, though, there's none of that. All assumptions, all conventional truths get ripped away. They all collapse. When the body is empty of self, what is there to latch onto? Physical elements, mental elements, they're already empty of any self. You have to see this clearly all the way through. Otherwise, they gather together and form a being, both physical and mental, and then you latch onto them as being your self.

Once we see the world as elements, however, there's no death. And once we can see that there's no death, that's when we'll really *know.* If we still see that we die, that shows that we haven't yet seen the Dhamma. We're still stuck on the outer shell. And when this is the case, what sort of Dhamma can we expect to know? You have to penetrate more deeply, to contemplate, taking things apart.

You're almost at the end of your lease in this burning house and yet you continue latching onto it as your self. It tricks you into feeling fear and love, and when you fall for it, what path will you practice? The mind latches onto these things to fool itself on many, many levels. You can't see through even *these* conventions, so you grasp hold of them as your self, as a woman, a man—and you really turn yourself into these things. If you can't contemplate so as to empty yourself of these conventions and assumptions, your practice simply circles around in the same old place, and as a result you can't find any way out.

So you have to contemplate down through many levels. It's like using a cloth to filter things. If you use a coarse weave, you won't catch much of anything. You have to use a fine weave to filter down to the deeper levels and penetrate *into* the deeper levels by contemplating over and over again, through level after level. That's why there are many levels to being mindful and discerning, filtering through to the details.

And this is why examining and becoming fully aware of your own inner character is so important. The practice of meditation is nothing but catching sight of self-deceptions, to see how they infiltrate into the deepest levels and how even the most blatant levels fool us right before our very eyes. If you can't catch sight of the deceits and deceptions of the self, your practice won't lead to release from suffering. It will simply keep you deluded into thinking that everything is you and yours.

To practice in line with the Buddha's teachings is to go *against* the flow. Every living being, deep down inside, wants pleasure on the physical level and then on the higher and more subtle levels of feeling, such as the types of concentration that are addicted to feelings of peace and respite. This is why you have to investigate into feeling so that you can let go of it and thus snuff out craving, through being fully aware of feeling as it actually is—free from any self—in line with its nature: unentangled, uninvolved. This is what snuffs out the virus of craving so that ultimately it vanishes without a trace.

THE INTRICACIES OF IGNORANCE

There are many layers to self-deception. The more you practice and investigate things, the less you feel like claiming to know. Instead, you'll simply see the harm of your own many-faceted ignorance and foolishness. Your examination of the viruses in the mind gets more and more subtle. Before, you didn't know, so you took your views to be knowledge—because you thought you knew. But actually these things aren't real knowledge. They're the type of understanding that comes from labels. Still we think they're knowledge and we think *we* know. This in itself is a very intricate self-deception.

So you have to keep watch on these things, to keep contemplating them. Sometimes they fool us right before our eyes: That's when it really gets bad, because we don't know that we've got ourselves fooled, and instead think we're people who know. We can deal thoroughly with this or that topic, but our knowledge is simply the memory of labels. We think that labels are discernment, or thought-formations are discernment, or the awareness of sensory consciousness is discernment, and so we get these things all mixed up. As a result, we become enamored with all the bits of knowledge that slip in and fashion the mind—which are simply the illusions within awareness. As for genuine awareness, there's very little of it, while deceptive awareness has us surrounded on all sides.

We thus have to contemplate and investigate so as to see through these illusions in awareness. This is what will enable us to read the mind. If your awareness goes out, don't follow it out. Stop and turn inward instead. Whatever slips in to fashion the mind, you have to be wise to it. You can't forbid it, for it's something natural, and you shouldn't try to close off the mind too much. Simply keep watch on awareness to see how far it will go, how true or false it is, how it disbands and then arises again. You have to watch it over and over again. Simply watching in this way will enable you to read yourself, to know cause and effect within yourself, and to contemplate yourself. This is what will make your mindfulness and discernment more and more skillful. If you don't practice in this way, the mind will be dark. It may get a little empty, a little still, and you'll decide that's plenty good enough.

But if you look at the Buddha's teachings, you'll find that no matter what sort of correct knowledge he gained, he was never willing to stop there. He always said, "There's more." To begin with, he developed mindfulness and clear comprehension in every activity, but then he said, "There's more to do, further to go." As for us, we're always ready to brag. We work at developing this or that factor for a while and then say we already know all about it and don't have to develop it any further. As a result, the principles in our awareness go soft *because of our boastfulness and pride.*

EMPTINESS vs. THE VOID

To open the door so that you can really see inside yourself isn't easy, but it's something you can train yourself to do. If you have the mindfulness enabling you to read yourself and understand yourself, that cuts through a lot of the issues right there. Craving will have a hard time forming. In whatever guise it arises, you'll get to read it, to know it, to extinguish it, to let it go.

When you get to do these things, it doesn't mean that you "get" anything, for actually once the mind is empty, that means it doesn't gain anything at all. But to put it into words for those who haven't experienced it: In what ways is emptiness empty? Does it mean that everything disappears or is annihilated? Actually, you should know that emptiness doesn't mean that the mind is annihilated. All that's annihilated is clinging and attachment. What you have to do is to see what emptiness is like as it actually appears and then not latch onto it. The nature of this emptiness is that it's deathless within you—this emptiness of self—and yet the mind can still function, know, and read itself. Just don't label it or latch onto it, that's all.

There are many levels to emptiness, many types, but if it's this or that type, then it's not genuine emptiness, for it contains the intention trying to know what type of emptiness it is, what features it has. This is something you have to look into deeply if you really want to know. If it's superficial emptiness—the emptiness of the still mind, free from thought-formations about its objects or free from the external sense of self—that's not genuine emptiness. Genuine emptiness lies deep, not on the level of mere stillness or concentration. The emptiness of the void is something very profound.

But because of the things we've studied and heard, we tend to label the emptiness of the still mind as the void—and so we label things wrongly in that emptiness.... Actually it's just ordinary stillness. We have to look more deeply in. No matter what you've encountered that you've heard about before, don't get excited. Don't label it as this or that level of attainment. Otherwise you'll spoil everything. You reach the level where you should be able to keep your awareness steady, but once you label things, it stops right there—or else goes all out of control.

This labeling is attachment in action. It's something very subtle, very refined. Whatever appears, it latches on. So you simply have to let the mind be empty without labeling it as anything, for the emptiness that lets go of preoccupations or is free from the influence of thought-formations *is something you have to look further into.* Don't label it as this or that level, for to measure and compare things in this way blocks everything—and in particular, knowledge of how the mind changes.

So to start out, simply watch these things, simply be aware. If you get excited, it ruins everything. Instead of seeing things clear through, you don't. You stop there and don't go any further. For this reason, when you train the mind or contemplate the mind to the point of gaining clear realizations every now and then, regard them as simply things to observe.

OPENING THE WAY IN THE HEART

Once you can read your mind correctly, you can catch hold of defilements and kill them off: That's insight meditation. The mind becomes razor sharp, just as if you have a sharp knife that can cut anything clear through. Even if defilements arise again, you can dig them up again, cut them off again. It's actually a lot of fun, this job of uprooting the defilements in the mind. There's no other work nearly as much fun as getting this sense of "I" or self under your thumb, because you get to see all of its tricks. It's really fun. Whenever it shows its face in order to get anything, you just watch it—to see what it wants and why it wants it, to see what inflated claims it makes for itself. This way you can cross-examine it and get to the facts.

Once you know, there's nothing to do but let go, to become unentangled and free. Just think of how good that can be! This practice of ours is a way of stopping and preventing all kinds of things inside ourselves. Whenever defilement rises up to get anything, to grab hold of anything, we don't play along. We let go. Just this is enough to do away with a lot of stress and suffering, even though the defilements feel the heat.

When we oppress the defilements a lot in this way, it gets them hot and feverish. But remember, it's the *defilements* that get hot and feverish. And remember that the Buddha told us to put the heat on the defilements, because if we don't put the heat on them, they put the heat on us all the time.

So we must be intent on burning the defilements away, even though they may complain that we're mistreating them. We close the door and imprison them. When they can't go anywhere, they're sure to complain: "I can't take it! I'm not free to go anywhere at all!" So simply watch them: Where do they want to go? What do they want to grab hold of? Where?

Watch them carefully, and they'll stop—stop going, stop running. It's easy to say no to other things, but saying no to yourself, saying no to your defilements, isn't easy at all—and yet it doesn't lie beyond your discernment or capabilities to do it. If you have the mindfulness and discernment to say no to defilement, it'll stop. Don't think that you can't make it stop. You *can* make it stop—simply that you've been foolish enough to give in to it so quickly that it's become second nature.

So we have to stop. Once we stop, the defilements can stop, too. Wherever they turn up, we can extinguish them. And when this is the case, how can we *not* want to practice? No matter how stubbornly they want anything, simply watch them. Get acquainted with them, and they won't stay. They'll disband. As soon as they disband, you realize exactly how deceptive they are. Before, you didn't know. As soon as they urged you to do anything, you went along with them. But once you're wise to them, they stop. They disband. Even though you don't disband them, they disband on their own. And as soon as you see their disbanding, the path opens wide before you. Everything opens wide in the heart. You can see that there's a way you can overcome defilement, you can put an end to defilement, no matter how much it arises. But you've got to remember to keep on watching out for it, keep on letting it go.

Thus I ask that you all make the effort to keep sharpening your tools at all times. Once your discernment is sharp on any point, it can let go of that point and uproot it. If you look after that state of mind and contemplate how to keep it going, you'll be able to keep your tools from growing dull.

And now that you know the basic principles, I ask that you make the effort to the utmost of your strength and mindfulness. May you be brave and resilient, so that your practice for gaining release from all your sufferings and stress can reap good results in every way.

Glossary

Aggregate *(khandha):* Physical and mental components of the personality and of sensory experience in general: Form (the body, any physical phenomenon); feeling; perception; thought-formations; and sensory consciousness.

Defilement *(kilesa):* Mental qualities that obscure the clarity of the mind. There are three basic sorts—passion, aversion, and delusion—but these can combine into a variety of forms. One standard list gives sixteen in all: greed, malevolence, anger, rancor, hypocrisy, arrogance, envy, miserliness, dishonesty, boastfulness, obstinacy, violence, pride, conceit, intoxication, and complacency.

Dhamma: Phenomenon; event; the way things are in and of themselves; their inherent qualities; the basic principles that underlie their behavior. Also, principles of behavior that human beings ought to follow so as to fit in with the right natural order of things; qualities of mind they should develop so as to realize the inherent quality of the mind in and of itself. By extension, "Dhamma" is used also to refer to any doctrine that teaches such things.

Effluent *(āsava):* Four qualities—sensuality, becoming, views, and ignorance—that flow out of the mind and create the flood of the round of death and rebirth.

Foundations of mindfulness *(satipaṭṭhāna):* The objects of concentration practice and contemplation—body, feelings, mind, and mental qualities as they are experienced in and of themselves.

Kamma: Intentional acts in thought, word, and deed that result in becoming and birth.

Name and form *(nāma-rūpa):* Mental and physical phenomena. "Form" is identical with the first aggregate (see above). "Name" covers the remaining four.

Nibbāna: Unbinding; the liberation of the mind from mental effluents, defilements, and the fetters that bind it to the round of rebirth. As this term is used to refer also to the extinguishing of fire, it carries the connotations of stilling, cooling, and peace. (According to the physics taught at the time of the Buddha, a burning fire seizes or adheres to its fuel; when extinguished, it is unbound.)

Noble Truths *(ariya-sacca):* The four categories for viewing experience in such a way that one can attain Awakening—stress, its cause, its disbanding, and the path of practice to its disbanding.

Soḷasa Pañhā: The Sixteen Questions, the final chapter in the Sutta Nipāta, in which sixteen young brahmins question the Buddha on subtle points of doctrine. Mogharāja's Question is the last of the sixteen.

THE BUDDHIST PUBLICATION SOCIETY

The BPS is an approved charity dedicated to making known the Teaching of the Buddha, which has a vital message for people of all creeds. Founded in 1958, the BPS has published a wide variety of books and booklets covering a great range of topics. Its publications include accurate annotated translations of the Buddha's discourses, standard reference works, as well as original contemporary expositions of Buddhist thought and practice. These works present Buddhism as it truly is—a dynamic force which has influenced receptive minds for the past 2500 years and is still as relevant today as it was when it first arose. A full list of our publications will be sent upon request with an enclosure of U.S. $1.50 or its equivalent to cover air mail postage. Write to:

The Hony. Secretary
BUDDHIST PUBLICATION SOCIETY
P.O. Box 61
54, Sangharaja Mawatha
Kandy • Sri Lanka